SUPERMAN
RED SON

MARK MILLAR
WRITER

DAVE JOHNSON & KILIAN PLUNKETT
PENCILLERS

ANDREW ROBINSON & WALDEN WONG
INKERS

PAUL MOUNTS COLORIST
KEN LOPEZ LETTERER
DAVE JOHNSON COVER PAINTER

SUPERMAN CREATED BY
JERRY SIEGEL & JOE SHUSTER

In Elseworlds, heroes are taken from their usual settings and put into strange times and places — some that have existed and others that can't, couldn't or shouldn't exist. The result is stories that make characters who are as familiar as yesterday seem as fresh as tomorrow.

DAN DIDIO VP-EDITORIAL
MIKE McAVENNIE & TOM PALMER JR. EDITORS-ORIGINAL SERIES
MAUREEN McTIGUE ASSISTANT EDITOR-ORIGINAL SEIES
ANTON KAWASAKI EDITOR-COLLECTED EDITION
AMIE BROCKWAY-METCALF ART DIRECTOR
PAUL LEVITZ PRESIDENT & PUBLISHER
GEORG BREWER VP-DESIGN & RETAIL PRODUCT DEVELOPMENT
RICHARD BRUNING SENIOR VP-CREATIVE DIRECTOR
PATRICK CALDON SENIOR VP-FINANCE & OPERATIONS
CHRIS CARAMALIS VP-FINANCE
TERRI CUNNINGHAM VP-MANAGING EDITOR
ALISON GILL VP-MANUFACTURING
LILLIAN LASERSON SENIOR VP & GENERAL COUNSEL
JIM LEE EDITORIAL DIRECTOR-WILDSTORM
DAVID MCKILLIPS VP-ADVERTISING & CUSTOM PUBLISHING
JOHN NEE VP-BUSINESS DEVELOPMENT
GREGORY NOVECK SENIOR VP-CREATIVE AFFAIRS
CHERYL RUBIN VP-BRAND MANAGEMENT
BOB WAYNE VP-SALES & MARKETING

SUPERMAN: RED SON

ISBN: 9781840238013

Published by Titan Books, a division of Titan Publishing Group Ltd., 144 Southwark Street, London SE1 0UP.
Cover, introduction and compilation copyright © 2004 DC Comics. All Rights Reserved.
Originally published in single magazine form in SUPERMAN: RED SON #1-3.

A CIP catalogue record for this book is available from the British Library.

Printed in Spain.
8 10 9

Cover painting by Dave Johnson
Logo design by Steve Cook

Mom, apple pie, Chevrolet, and SUPERMAN.

INTRODUCTION BY TOM DeSANTO

LET OUR ENEMIES BEWARE:

THERE IS ONLY **ONE** SUPERPOWER NOW.

With all due respect to Mickey Mouse, there is perhaps no greater American icon than the Man of Steel. When Mark Millar first told me the premise of RED SON — of taking the American icon of Superman and putting him in the ultimate what-if scenario — I was shocked. Imagine Superman wasn't red, white, and blue …imagine Superman was red… Communist red? Instead of baby Kal-El landing in the loving arms of Ma and Pa Kent in the good ol' U.S. of A., he lands in the loving arms of Josef Stalin back in the U.S.S.R. No longer Superman American icon, but Superman Soviet comrade — needless to say, the premise is more than intriguing. In the hands of a lesser writer the story would have fallen into cookie cutter, black and white, America good, Soviets bad, feel-good propaganda. Thank God Mark Millar is not a lesser writer. And thank God his favorite color seems to be gray.

All that morally questionable gray is captured in what seems to be 1950s Technicolor glory. Fortunately the artistic palette of Dave Johnson's and Kilian Plunkett's pencils, Andrew Robinson's and Walden Wong's inks, and Paul Mount's colors combine to create a Kafkaesque, Max Fleischer cartoon that collides with the best of propaganda art. It is not like you are reading a graphic novel but watching a movie. This book is everything I love about comics — a great morality tale with art that leaps off the page and into your mind's eye.

Even if you have never read a comic before, you can pick up RED SON and follow the story and enjoy a great ride. But don't be fooled; it is much more than that. RED SON is a sharp social commentary on capitalism vs. communism and current American foreign policy. Not bad for a funny book. If you are a comic fan, then you will notice the detail to the Superman mythology. Having read the book three times, I find such an attention to detail that I am still discovering something new in the words or art that I somehow had missed

CITIZENS! ALL HAIL OUR COMRADE OF STEEL

AND THE WORKER'S UTOPIA!

before. All the elements that make Superman great are there: Lex Luthor, Lois Lane (oops, I mean Lois *Luthor*), Jimmy Olsen, even Batman, Wonder Woman, and the greatest Green Lantern of them all, Hal Jordan. All of them the same, yet different — all reinvented. Even though the traditional "S" on his chest has been replaced by the hammer and sickle, one thing is still the same — Superman believes he is doing the right thing. He has the best of intentions, but we all know what the road to hell is paved with. Yet Superman still wants to make the world safe, except this time he is willing to force us to see that his way is the best way.

Ben Franklin once wrote, "Those who would sacrifice their freedom for safety will find they inherit neither." That line, written over two hundred years ago, may have more meaning now than ever before. Good writing challenges the way you think. Great writing *changes* the way you think. RED SON is great writing. Mark actually started writing RED SON around 1995, and we all know it is a much different world than those days. Millar was able to gaze into his Orwellian crystal ball and see Superman as the poster child for Big Brother. The all X-ray vision seeing, all super-hearing listening, all-knowing, all-powerful Big Brother. All-encompassing security, like a baby in a super blanket — just one thing…don't think for yourself and don't challenge the system. Free will or freedom in exchange for absolute security — I don't think Ben Franklin would have liked that idea. Just remember Superman is watching you. But who's watching the watchmen? Mark Millar is, that's who.

Be good,
Tom DeSanto
OCTOBER 9, 2003

A self-described pop culture junkie and longtime comic book fan, Tom DeSanto is a writer/producer who has worked on various films such as Apt Pupil, X-Men *and* X2: X-Men United, *among other projects. He currently lives in Los Angeles.*

IN THE MIDDLE OF THE **TWENTIETH CENTURY**, THE TELEPHONES STARTED RINGING ALL ACROSS AMERICA AS **RUMORS** OF MY EXISTENCE STARTED **CIRCULATING.**

EVEN IN THOSE **DIM AND DISTANT DAYS**, I COULD HEAR THE **INSECT BUZZ** OF A **MILLION CONVERSATIONS** FROM CALIFORNIA TO METROPOLIS AND **BACK** AGAIN.

AN **ENTIRE CONTINENT** WAS WAKING UP TO REALIZE THAT THEIR LIVES WERE SOON TO CHANGE **FOREVER.**

BRRRIIIIINNNNNGGG

BRRRIIIIINNNNNGGG

KLKKLLKKLLK

LOIS **LANE**. I MEAN, **LUTHOR**. LOIS **LUTHOR.**

OH, DON'T BE SUCH A **JERK**, CHIEF. IT'S **SIX A.M.** AND SOME OF US HAVE **SOCIAL LIVES**. NO, WE **HAVEN'T** HEARD THE RADIO. WHAT'S **HAPPENED?**

WHO KNOWS, SWEETHEART?

EITHER THE **RUSSIANS** JUST INVADED **IDAHO** OR J. EDGAR HOOVER LIKES TO DRESS IN **LADIES' LINGERIE**, BECAUSE WASHINGTON JUST CALLED AND PROMISED US THE **STORY** OF THE **CENTURY.**

IKE'S MAKING A BROADCAST LIVE FROM THE OVAL OFFICE AT LUNCH TIME ON A MATTER OF **GRAVE NATIONAL IMPORTANCE.**

WHAT'S THE **INSIDE SCOOP?** WELL, BETWEEN **YOU AND ME**, KID, RUMOR HAS IT THE SOVIETS JUST DEVELOPED A BRAND-NEW KIND OF **SUPER-WEAPON.**

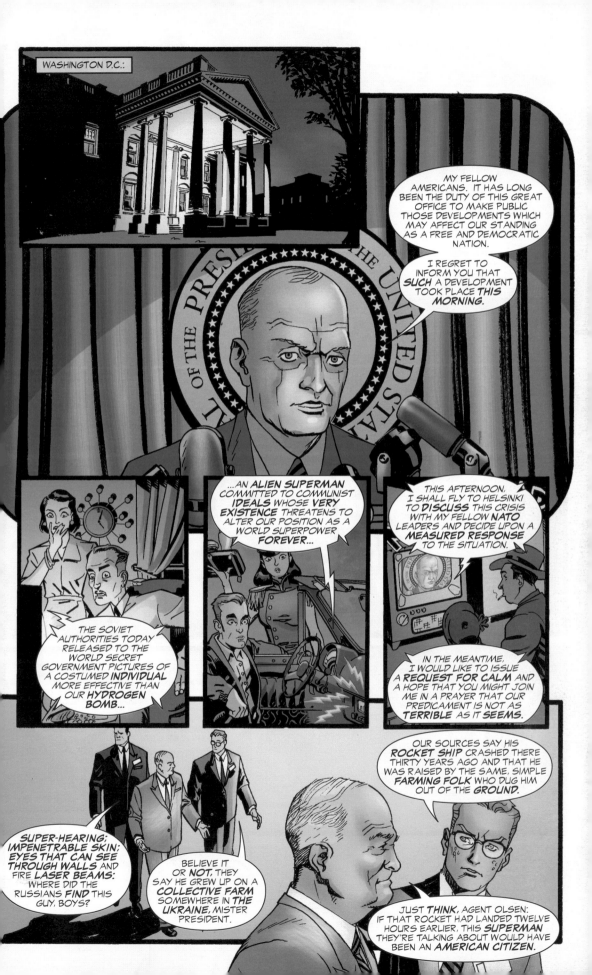

GREAT CAESAR'S GHOST! SUPERMAN SPOTTED IN DENVER! SUPERMAN SIGHTED IN NEBRASKA! SUPERMAN SEEN HOVERING OVER A FIELD IN ARKANSAS!

WHAT THE HELL'S GOING ON HERE, LOIS? IT'S LIKE THE WHOLE DAMN COUNTRY'S SEEING RED CAPES UNDER THEIR BEDS.

PERRY WHITE
EDITOR IN CHIEF

WARS OVER

PENTAGON JUST CONFIRMED THREE MORE SUPER-POWERS, CHIEF; STRENGTH, SPEED AND FLIGHT. RECEPTIONIST ALSO ADDED SUPER-BREATH WHEN I OFFERED HER TWENTY BUCKS.

SUPER-BREATH? WHAT IN GOD'S NAME IS SUPER-BREATH? IS EVERYBODY ON THIS PLANET GOING NUTS?

THAT'S ABSOLUTELY CORRECT, SIR. I WAS JUST COMING OFF-DUTY WHEN I SAW A HUMAN-SHAPED FIGURE ZIP PAST ME AND THEN I HEARD LAUGHING UP THERE IN THE CLOUDS.

THEY SAY HE CAN SEE US FROM SPACE WITH THOSE SUPER-EYES OF HIS AND THAT HE'S WATCHING OUR EVERY MOVE, JUST BIDING HIS TIME FOR THE PERFECT MOMENT TO STRIKE.

RUMOR HAS IT HIS BOSSES BACK IN MOSCOW ARE PUSHING FOR A FULL-BLOWN INVASION IN A MATTER OF WEEKS NOW.

WGSX

KENT
HARDWARE

HECK, THE WHOLE COUNTRY'S LINING THEIR WALLS WITH LEAD, MARTHA. WE CAN'T HAVE SUPERMAN WATCHING US ON THE TOILET WITH THAT HORRIBLE X-RAY VISION OF HIS, NOW CAN WE?

THE GOOD PEOPLE OF SMALLVILLE HAVE THEIR DIGNITY TO THINK OF.

OH MY LORD. AIN'T IT ENOUGH THEY GOT THEIR SATELLITES AND ENOUGH NUCLEAR BOMBS TO BLOW US ALL UP TEN TIMES OVER WITHOUT STALIN'S SUPER-SPACEMAN TOO?

I JUST THANK MY LUCKY STARS DEAR, SWEET JONATHAN NEVER LIVED TO SEE THE DAY THIS COUNTRY WOULD BE BROUGHT TO ITS KNEES LIKE THIS.

HAD MADE QUITE AN *IMPRESSION* IN THE FOURTEEN WEEKS SINCE I'D MADE MY JOURNEY FROM THE FARM LANDS TO MOSCOW.

OME STILL THOUGHT ME A *TRICK OF THE LIGHT* OR AN *URBAN MYTH*, BUT EACH NEW DAY SAW ANOTHER *SUPER-FEAT* OR SOME *DEATH-DEFYING RESCUE*.

N MY MORE *INTROSPECTIVE* MOMENTS, I EVEN WONDERED IF PEOPLE WERE BEHAVING MORE CARELESSLY IN THE HOPE THAT THEY MIGHT CATCH A *GLIMPSE* OF THEIR *GAUDY CIRCUS CLOWN*.

COMRADE SECRETARY, THIS IS A PRIORITY ALERT! WE HAVE LOST CONTROL OF *SPUTNIK TWO* AND THE SATELLITE IS PLUMMETING TOWARDS *EARTH'S* ATMOSPHERE!

THE *AMERICANS!* THEY MUST HAVE *SABOTAGED* US! HOW ELSE COULD A SATELLITE JUST *CHANGE COURSE* LIKE THAT?

FLIGHT TRAJECTORY LOOKS LIKE IT'S HEADING FOR A *POPULATED AREA* SOMEWHERE IN THE UPPER HEMISPHERE, SIR. *NORTH* OF PERU, *NORTH* OF CUBA--

OH MY GOD! IT'S COMING DOWN

THEY CALLED ME A *SOLDIER*, BUT THAT JUST *WASN'T TRUE*.

I WAS *NEVER* A SOLDIER.

A SOLDIER *ALWAYS* FOLLOWS ORDERS. A SOLDIER *KNOWS* AND *HATES* HIS ENEMY. A SOLDIER ONLY *FIGHTS* AND *DIES* FOR HIS *OWN PEOPLE*...

I JUST FOUGHT FOR WHAT WAS *RIGHT*.

Sputnik Two weighed five thousand pounds.

This mass multiplied by an acceleration factor of a **hundred meters per second** would have delivered a force powerful enough to level the **entire city**.

In hindsight, there are **so many ways** this predicament might have been **solved**.

BAKK!

I could have **vaporized** it with my **heat vision**, slowed its descent with my **super-breath** or even **atomized** the craft with a **calculated blow**.

Instead, I chose the most **exciting** action.

THOOOM!

The powers were still **new** to me then, you understand.

EXACTLY THREE SECONDS AFTER HITTING THE ROOF OF THE *NEWSPAPER OFFICE*, I REALIZED THE DAMAGE DONE TO THE *BUILDING'S SUSPENSION.*

METROPOLIS WAS ALIVE WITH *NOISE* AGAIN, BUT I COULD STILL HEAR LOOSE BRICKS START TO FALL *TWO MILES WEST.*

A CLUSTER OF SUPPORT CABLES *GROANED* AND *SNAPPED.* PEOPLE BELOW SCREAMED FOR *SOMEONE* TO *SAVE* THEM.

SKRRRR!

NOT *MY* PEOPLE...

BUT I *NEVER* REFUSE A CRY FOR HELP.

ALL THE *LIES* THEY SPREAD ABOUT ME. THE *PROPAGANDA* THEY ENGINEERED AT THE HEIGHT OF THE *COLD WAR.* NONE OF IT *MATTERED* FOR A WHILE ON THAT *BRIGHT AFTERNOON.*

JUST FOR A *SINGLE MOMENT.*

THEY REALIZED I WAS HERE TO SAVE THEM.

OH. MY. GOD.

SIX MILLION *LIVES* SPARED AND AN INCIDENT THAT MIGHT HAVE SPARKED A WAR *AVERTED* AND MY MOST POTENT MEMORY OF THAT DAY WAS FIVE AND A HALF FEET TALL AND WEARING CHANEL NO 5.

SHE FELT IT *TOO*. I *KNOW* SHE DID; FROM THE INCREASE IN HER *PULSE RATE* TO THE MICRON OF EXTRA *PERSPIRATION* ON HER SKIN, BUT NEITHER OF US COULD *ACT* ON THIS IMPULSE.

NOT WHILE SHE HAD A *GOLD RING* ON HER *THIRD FINGER* AND A *CREASED PHOTOGRAPH* OF A SOMBRE, *RED-HEADED SCIENTIST* IN HER PURSE.

CENTURIES LATER, AFTER A *THOUSAND INTERPRE-TATIONS* OF THIS MEETING, A FAMOUS POET WOULD WRITE AN ALTERNATE HISTORY OF THE WORLD WHERE *LOIS LUTHOR* AND I BECAME *LOVERS*.

HIS STORY WOULD GO ON TO WIN *THE PULITZER PRIZE* AND BECOME THE *BIGGEST-SELLING FICTIONAL BOOK* OF ALL TIME.

EVEN *NOW*, I STILL DON'T KNOW WHAT APPEALS TO PEOPLE ABOUT THIS NOTION, WHAT *CHORD* IT STRUCK WITH THE *PUBLIC IMAGINATION*...

23

...AND I DON'T SUPPOSE WE EVER WILL IN *THIS* LIFETIME.

The ELECTRICAL BREAKFAST

Electric Compendium

MAGNIFICENT, ISN'T HE? ABSOLUTELY *MAGNIFICENT.* I *KNEW* THESE RANDOM ACTS OF HEROISM WOULDN'T BE CONFINED TO THE PARAMETERS OF *MOTHER RUSSIA.*

IT'S SUCH A *SHAME* HE WORKS FOR THE OTHER SIDE. I HONESTLY BELIEVE THAT SUPERMAN AND I WOULD HAVE BEEN THE *BEST OF FRIENDS* IF HE'D POPPED UP IN *AMERICA.*

WHAT MADE YOU SO SURE HE'D ACTUALLY BE ABLE TO *SAVE* US, DOCTOR LUTHOR?

MATHEMATICS, OLSEN. PURE *MATHEMATICS.*

NOW MAKE SURE THEY RAISE THAT SATELLITE FROM THE WATER PRECISELY AS I *DESCRIBED.* THE INFORMATION HE LEFT ON THAT *HULL* IS *ESSENTIAL...*

ESPECIALLY IF OUR DEAR FRIEND IN THE WHITE HOUSE EXPECTS ME TO BUILD HIM A *SUPERMAN* OF OUR *OWN.*

WEEKS PASS AND A THOUSAND RESCUES LATER, THEY DECIDED TO THROW A *WELCOME PARADE* FOR ME.

I CAN REMEMBER EVERY SINGLE, SILLY *DETAIL* OF THAT DAY IN *RED SQUARE*. EVERY *FACE* IN THE *CROWD*. EVERY *PIMPLE* ON EVERY FACE OF EVERY CHEERING WORKER...

THEIR POOR, CONFUSED *EXPRESSIONS* AT THIS *CHAMPION* FROM THE *FARM LANDS* WHO COULDN'T *STAND STILL* FOR MORE THAN TEN SECONDS AT A TIME.

DON'T TELL ME THERE'S *ANOTHER* EMERGENCY, SUPERMAN...

A *CHEMICAL PLANT* ON FIRE THREE THOUSAND MILES WEST OF *VLADIVOSTOK*, COMRADE STALIN. JUST GIVE ME TEN OR *FIFTEEN* MINUTES.

OKAY, BUT DON'T BE ANY *LONGER*.

THIS *SUPERMAN DAY* THING IS SUPPOSED TO BE FOR *YOU*, YOU KNOW.

HE'S GOT THE *ATTENTION SPAN* OF A *SPASTIC TWO-YEAR-OLD*, HASN'T HE? IMAGINE NOT EVEN BEING ABLE TO SIT THROUGH YOUR OWN *DAMN PARADE*.

WELL, WHAT'S HE *SUPPOSED* TO DO, CAPTAIN? STAND THERE AND GRIN LIKE AN IDIOT WHEN HE CAN *HEAR* PEOPLE *SCREAMING* FOR *THEIR LIVES*?

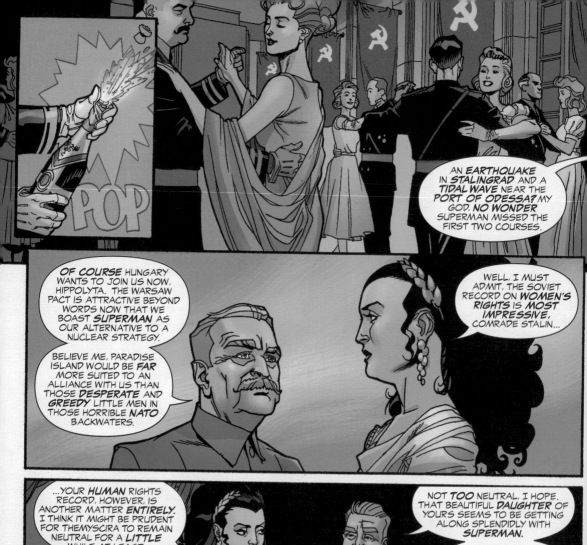

POP

AN EARTHQUAKE IN **STALINGRAD** AND A **TIDAL WAVE** NEAR THE **PORT OF ODESSA?** MY GOD, **NO WONDER** SUPERMAN MISSED THE FIRST TWO COURSES.

OF COURSE HUNGARY WANTS TO JOIN US NOW, HIPPOLYTA. THE WARSAW PACT IS ATTRACTIVE BEYOND WORDS NOW THAT WE BOAST **SUPERMAN** AS OUR ALTERNATIVE TO A NUCLEAR STRATEGY.

BELIEVE ME, PARADISE ISLAND WOULD BE **FAR** MORE SUITED TO AN ALLIANCE WITH US THAN THOSE **DESPERATE** AND **GREEDY** LITTLE MEN IN THOSE HORRIBLE **NATO** BACKWATERS.

WELL, I MUST ADMIT, THE SOVIET RECORD ON **WOMEN'S RIGHTS** IS **MOST** IMPRESSIVE, COMRADE STALIN...

...YOUR **HUMAN** RIGHTS RECORD, HOWEVER, IS ANOTHER MATTER **ENTIRELY.** I THINK IT MIGHT BE PRUDENT FOR THEMYSCIRA TO REMAIN NEUTRAL FOR A **LITTLE** WHILE AT LEAST.

NOT **TOO** NEUTRAL, I HOPE. THAT BEAUTIFUL **DAUGHTER** OF YOURS SEEMS TO BE GETTING ALONG SPLENDIDLY WITH **SUPERMAN.**

I THOUGHT, PERHAPS, THAT YOU AND I MIGHT GET **SIMILARLY ACQUAINTED** UPSTAIRS IN THE **PRESIDENTIAL SUITE?**

PLEASE. DON'T EMBARRASS YOURSELF, JOSEPH.

MAYBE IF YOU WERE **FIVE THOUSAND** YEARS OLDER...

WHAT'S **WRONG,** SUPERMAN? YOU LOOK SO **SAD.** I HOPE THIS ISN'T ANYTHING TO DO WITH MY TERRIBLE **RUSSIAN.**

NO, NOT AT **ALL,** DIANA. YOU'RE ACTUALLY **WORD PERFECT.** IT'S JUST THIS WHOLE **SUPERMAN DAY** FUSS: **PARTIES** AND **PARADES** JUST AREN'T REALLY **ME.**

I **KNOW** WHAT YOU **MEAN.** THERE'S ALWAYS SOMETHING BEING HELD IN MY HONOR BACK ON **PARADISE ISLAND** TOO, SO I KNOW HOW **TIRESOME** THESE THINGS ARE.

WELL, I HOPE **TONIGHT** ISN'T TOO BORING FOR YOU.

GREAT HERA, NO! NOT IN THE **SLIGHTEST.** I'M ACTUALLY HAVING A **WONDERFUL** TIME. I MEAN, **THINK** ABOUT IT: HOW OFTEN DO I GET TO MEET **SOMEONE** LIKE **ME?**

I SEE **SOMEONE'S** ENJOYING HERSELF, EH? BUILDING BRIDGES WITH THE **FUTURE LEADER,** ARE YOU?

OH, SUPERMAN'S REALLY **NICE,** MOTHER. YOU SHOULD **TALK** TO HIM. HE'S REALLY NOT LIKE OTHER MEN **AT ALL,** YOU KNOW. HE SEEMS A FEW INCHES **TALLER.**

THAT *DIANA* WOULD MAKE A FINE WIFE WHEN SHE MAKES HER VOYAGE TO THE *MAN'S WORLD*, SUPERMAN. JUST IMAGINE WHAT KIND OF *CHILDREN* YOU COULD RAISE, EH?

HAVEN'T WE BEEN HERE *ALREADY*, COMRADE STALIN? I DIDN'T *COME* HERE TO BREED.

BUT THINK ABOUT THE *FUTURE*, MY BOY. THE DYNASTY OF *SUPERMEN* THAT COULD PRESERVE OUR IDEALS *FOREVER*.

BESIDES, IS THERE ANOTHER WOMAN IN ALL THE WORLD WHO COULD... AH... *KEEP UP* WITH OUR WONDERFUL *MAN OF STEEL*?

I'D PREFER TO CHOOSE MY *OWN* WIFE, COMRADE STALIN. BESIDES, THIS NOTION YOU HAVE THAT I'D EVER WANT TO LEAD THE PARTY IS REALLY QUITE A *MISCONCEPTION*.

POLITICS BORES ME *RIGID*. I ONLY CAME TO THE *BIG CITY* SO THAT I COULD USE MY POWERS TO *HELP* PEOPLE.

UH, WHY ARE YOU STARING AT THE *WALL*, SUPERMAN?

I'M SCANNING MOSCOW FOR YOUR *CHIEF OF POLICE*, SIR. I NOTICED HE ISN'T AT THE PARTY AND I JUST WANTED TO MAKE SURE HE'S *OKAY*. THERE'S NO SIGN OF HIM *ANYWHERE*.

OH, FOR GOD'S SAKE. WHO CARES ABOUT *PYOTR ROSLOV*?

I CARE ABOUT *EVERYBODY*, SIR.

AH, *THERE* HE IS; TWO HUNDRED MILES AWAY ON THE PEASANT LAND WHERE *HE* GREW UP. YOU'LL HAVE TO *EXCUSE* ME FOR A MOMENT, COMRADE...

CATCH.

ACTUALLY, THE **POWERS** DIDN'T START UNTIL A FEW WEEKS AFTER MY **TWELFTH BIRTHDAY**, CAPTAIN ROSLOV.

MY **SUPER-HEARING** WAS THE FIRST TO DEVELOP. I HEARD WHAT I THOUGHT WERE **VOICES** IN MY **HEAD** UNTIL I REALIZED I WAS JUST LISTENING TO CHILDREN IN THE **NEXT COLLECTIVE.**

UP UNTIL THAT POINT, I WAS JUST AN ORDINARY LITTLE BOY WITH BRUISED KNEES AND A WHEEZY COUGH AND A CRUSH ON MY CUTE, RED-HEADED NEIGHBOR JUST LIKE **ANYONE ELSE.**

IF I'D HAD THE **POWERS** I'D HAVE LEFT THE FARM **YEARS** BEFORE NOW, BUT I DIDN'T. YOU KNOW WHY?

BECAUSE MY **PARENTS** WANTED ME TO BE **READY** WHEN I WENT TO THE BIG CITY. I BELIEVE IN THIS JUST AS MUCH AS **YOU** DO, PYOTR. THIS DOESN'T HAVE TO BE A **COMPETITION.**

THAT'S EASY TO SAY WHEN YOU'RE STREAKING THROUGH THE **SKIES,** SUPERMAN. NOT SO MUCH FUN WHEN YOU'RE DOWN HERE WORKING IN THE **GUTTERS** LIKE THE **REST** OF US.

DON'T *WALK*.

RUN!

CHUNT!

WEIRD LITTLE *RUNT*.

PROBABLY GROW UP JUST LIKE HIS IDIOT *FATHER*.

THE KID COULDN'T HAVE BEEN MORE THAN NINE YEARS OLD, BUT HIS GLARE WOULD HAVE STOPPED A *CLOCK* TICKING. THOSE WEREN'T A *CHILD'S* EYES. THEY LOOKED TOO *PATIENT*.

I WILL NEVER, EVER FORGET THE WAY THAT BOY *STARED* AT ME.

SOMEBODY SAID HE THREW HIMSELF IN THE *MOSCOW RIVER*. OTHERS SAID HE DISAPPEARED INTO THE SEWERS TO *LICK HIS WOUNDS* AND SWEAR *REVENGE*.

I SHOT HIS *PARENTS*. WHAT DOES THAT *DO* TO A BOY, SUPERMAN? IS THERE ANYBODY WHO CAN ANSWER *THAT* ONE?

YOU KNOW, YOU'RE REALLY GOING TO *HURT* YOURSELF SOON IF YOU DON'T CUT OUT ALL THIS *HEAVY DRINKING,* PYOTR.

DAMN *YOU!*

THEY ALL MIGHT THINK YOU'RE WONDERFUL *NOW,* BUT I KNOW WHERE THIS IS *GOING,* ALIEN! YOUR *INTERFERENCE* IS GOING TO BE THE WORST THING THAT EVER *HAPPENED* TO US.

YOU *MARK MY WORDS!*

OH, JESUS.

I'VE DONE SUCH A *TERRIBLE THING,* SUPERMAN. FATHER MADE ME SO *ANGRY* THIS MORNING AND I ARRANGED--

WHAT?

I SAID...

NO, NOT *YOU. TWO MILES AWAY.* THERE'S SOMEONE SHOUTING FOR HELP IN *MOSCOW.*

WAIT HERE.

THE DAYS AND WEEKS THAT FOLLOWED SAW AMERICA **RUTHLESSLY EXPLOIT** OUR **POLITICAL CONFUSION.**

I LISTENED TO THEM AS THEY **PLOTTED** IN THEIR **BUNKERS** AND RECOGNIZED TO MY **HORROR** THAT THE COLD WAR HAD JUST DIPPED BELOW **FREEZING POINT.**

THEIR FIRST ACT WAS A PROMISE TO **CONTAIN** THE COMMUNIST THREAT BY INCREASING THEIR NUCLEAR STOCKPILES IN THE **UNITED KINGDOM** AND OUR VARIOUS **SATELLITE COUNTRIES.**

THIS PROMISE WAS LATER ENFORCED BY **OFFICIAL CONFIRMATION** THAT THE UNITED STATES OF AMERICA HAD DEVELOPED A **DUPLICATE SUPERMAN** OF THEIR **OWN.**

STALIN'S DEATH HAD LEFT AN ENORMOUS **VOID** IN OUR GREAT NATION THAT THE PARTY HIERARCHY BEGGED ME TO **FILL.** HOWEVER, THIS WAS A RESCUE I WAS **RELUCTANT** TO **UNDERTAKE...**

WHY SHOULD THE FACT THAT I WAS **BORN** WITH **PRIVILEGES** QUALIFY ME AS LEADER OF A **SOCIALIST REPUBLIC?**

I'M **SORRY,** COMRADES, BUT THE VERY **IDEA** OF THIS IS IN COMPLETE CONTRADICTION TO EVERYTHING WE WERE EVER RAISED TO **BELIEVE** IN.

THE DUPLICATE WAS *IMPERFECT*. A CRUDE EFFORT COMPARED TO LEX'S *LATER* WORK WITH ABILITIES LITTLE MORE THAN A *WARPED AGGREGATE* OF MY *OWN* REPERTOIRE...

...*LIKE TELESCOPIC X-RAY VISION*.

NOSES BLED. HEADS POUNDED. BIRDS BECAME IRRADIATED AND DROPPED FROM THE SKIES FOR FIFTY MILES AROUND. THE EFFECTS WERE DEVASTATING.

ABSOLUTELY DEVASTATING.

ENGAGE

THE SUBMARINE WAS A GRAYBACK CLASS SSG 574 CARRYING FOUR REGULUS ONE MISSILES.

THREE OF THEM STAYED WHERE THEY SHOULD HAVE.

GOOD GOD!

ENGLAND. LONDON. OXFORD STREET AND TWO HUNDRED AND FIFTY-EIGHT INNOCENT BY-STANDERS ARE DEAD BEFORE I EVEN HIT THE GROUND.

EVEN NOW. EVEN AFTER ALL THESE YEARS. I CAN STILL HEAR THE SOUND OF THEM SNAP.

A SECOND LATER.

ONE SINGLE SECOND...

...AND THE BODY COUNT TRIPLED.

SUDDENLY, THE **CLOCK** STOPPED.

TIME GROUND TO A HALT AS IT **ALWAYS** DOES FOR OUR KIND WHEN A DECISION MUST BE MADE.

THE DUPLICATE AND I **EXCHANGED** GLANCES, TWO **MOVING** OBJECTS ON A STATIC, FROZEN **BACKGROUND.**

WE BOTH KNEW THAT **ONE** OF US WOULD HAVE TO MAKE A **CHOICE.**

TO THIS DAY, HIS TRUE INTENTIONS REMAIN A **MYSTERY** TO ME.

THE END IS NIGH

US

I OFTEN WONDER IF HE REALLY KNEW WHAT HE WAS *DOING* WHEN HE KICKED BACK INTO THE SKY...

...OR IF HE UNDERSTOOD PERFECTLY AND *SACRIFICED* HIMSELF, INHERITING MY PROMISE TO PRESERVE *EVERY* FORM OF LIFE.

HELLO, EVERYBODY. ME VERY PLEASED TO *MEET* YOU.

PERHAPS HE LOOKED INTO MY EYES AND GLIMPSED A FUTURE THAT HE COULDN'T *BEAR* TO SEE, CHOOSING INSTEAD TO SPARE HIMSELF THE *SUFFERING.*

I'M AFRAID WE'LL NEVER *KNOW* FOR SURE.

CIRCLED THE WORLD AS I **OFTEN** DID WHEN TROUBLED: THE LAND, THE SEA AND THE MOUNTAINS BLURRING INTO A SINGLE STRETCH OF **ENDLESS GREY** BENEATH ME.

ALWAYS FOUND IT EASIEST TO THINK WHEN APPROACHING **TRANS-LIGHT** VELOCITIES.

MY HEART TOLD ME TO **LEAD** THEM, BUT MY HEAD TOLD ME THAT THIS **COMPLETELY CONTRADICTED** EVERYTHING MY PARENTS HAD EVER RAISED ME TO **BELIEVE** IN.

IT'S STRANGE HOW **DIFFERENT** THINGS COULD HAVE BEEN, THE PATH HISTORY MIGHT HAVE TAKEN IF I'D ONLY ENTERED MOSCOW FROM THE **NORTH SIDE** OF THE CITY...

RUSSIA WILL PROV

SUPERMAN?

LANA? LANA **LAZARENKO?**

I **THOUGHT** I HEARD YOU IN THE CROWDS EARLIER, BUT I COULDN'T BE SURE WITH ALL THE **CHATTERING** GOING ON.

MY GOD. **LOOK** AT YOU. YOU HAVEN'T CHANGED A **BIT** SINCE WE USED TO CAUSE ALL THAT TROUBLE ON THE FARM.

ME? WHAT ABOUT **YOU?** I NEARLY **DIED** WHEN THE CHILDREN SHOWED ME YOUR PICTURE IN THE PAPER. YOU WOULDN'T **BELIEVE** HOW HARD IT'S BEEN NOT TO TELL EVERYONE WHO YOU REALLY ARE.

CHILDREN?

YES, **JORDAN** AND **MEHRI.** WE SPENT ALL OUR MONEY TRAVELING FROM SAINT PETERSBURG FOR THE FUNERAL AND NOW WE HAVE TO QUEUE HERE FOR SCRAPS WITH **EVERYONE ELSE.**

THIS ISN'T *RIGHT*, LANA. THESE CHILDREN SHOULDN'T HAVE TO STAND IN LINE AND BEG FOR FOOD LIKE THEY'RE SOME KIND OF *ANIMALS*.

GIVE THIS WOMAN SOMETHING TO *EAT*, COMRADE. HER BOY AND GIRL HAVEN'T EATEN SINCE THEY *GOT* HERE, FOR GOD'S SAKE.

BUT WHAT ABOUT *US*, SUPERMAN? WE'RE *ALL* HUNGRY AND MY OWN CHILDREN HERE HAVEN'T EATEN ALL DAY *EITHER*.

SOME OF US HAVEN'T EATEN IN *WEEKS*.

THINGS ARE ONLY GOING TO GET WORSE NOW THAT *STALIN'S* DEAD *TOO*. I'VE GOT A FRIEND IN SUPPLIES WHO SAYS WE AREN'T GETTING *GRAINS* FOR THE REST OF THE *MONTH*.

IT'S *OKAY*, SUPERMAN. IT'S NOT *YOUR* FAULT. IT'S JUST THE WAY THE SYSTEM *WORKS*, YOU KNOW. YOU CAN'T TAKE CARE OF *EVERYONE'S* PROBLEMS.

ACTUALLY, I *CAN*, LANA. I *COULD* TAKE CARE OF EVERYONE'S PROBLEMS IF I *RAN* THIS PLACE AND, TO TELL YOU THE TRUTH, THERE'S NO GOOD REASON WHY I *SHOULDN'T*.

GAME OVER, LUTHOR.

FIFTY-EIGHT SECONDS? YOU'RE *SLOWING DOWN,* SUPERMAN. BRAINIAC'S SHIP WAS ONLY FORTY-FIVE THOUSAND MILES AWAY.

SURELY ADVANCING MIDDLE AGE ISN'T CATCHING UP WITH RUSSIA'S MIGHTY *MAN OF TOMORROW?*

BRAINIAC'S *CENTRAL PROCESSING UNIT,* LEX. I USED IT TO ACCESS EVERY FILE IN THE SHIP'S DATABASE, BUT THERE ISN'T A *SHRED* OF *USEFUL INFORMATION.*

I CAN'T FIND *ANY MEANS* OF RETURNING *STALINGRAD* TO ITS *NATURAL SIZE.*

HARDLY SURPRISING WHEN BRAINIAC'S PRIME DIRECTIVE WAS *STORING* INFORMATION ON ALIEN CULTURES. I DON'T THINK HE EVER INTENDED GIVING ANY OF THESE CITIES *BACK,* YOU KNOW.

TELL YOU *WHAT.* I'M ALWAYS READING HOW *SMART* YOU ARE. HOW NOTHING WE *MORTALS* CAN IMAGINE IS BEYOND *PRESIDENT SUPERMAN'S* LIMITATIONS, CORRECT?

WELL, NOW'S YOUR CHANCE TO PROVE THEM *RIGHT,* ALIEN.

BEST OF LUCK.

TEMPER, TEMPER, SUPERMAN.

HARDLY THE BEHAVIOR ONE WOULD EXPECT WHEN A *FOREIGN HEAD OF STATE* PAYS A VISIT TO AMERICA'S MOST ENTERPRISING *CORPORATION.*

CONTACT *THE BUILDERS. STANDARD* REPAIR.

OH, AND TELL *LOOMIS AND SCHOTT* I'M READY FOR ATTACK PLAN *THREE HUNDRED AND SEVEN,* MISS TESCHMACHER. I FEEL LIKE I'M ON AN INTELLECTUAL *ROLL* TODAY.

KNIGHT TO B3, INCIDENTALLY. THAT'S A *CHECKMATE,* TABLE EIGHTY-ONE.

MOSCOW:

--AND SO THIS MARKED THE END OF THE SHORT-LIVED *LUTHOR-BRAINIAC* PARTNERSHIP, BUT ONLY THE BEGINNING FOR THE TRAGIC PEOPLE OF *STALINGRAD.*

TO THIS *DAY,* OUR GREAT LEADER HAS BEEN UNABLE TO SOLVE THEIR PREDICAMENT, AND THEIR NAMES ARE ETCHED HERE FOREVER IN THE *SUPERMAN MUSEUM* SO THAT WE MIGHT *NEVER* FORGET.

OVER THE YEARS, THE AMERICAN C.I.A. HAS FUNDED THE CONSTRUCTION OF AN ENTIRE *ROGUES GALLERY* OF SUPER-CRIMINALS BUILT BY THE PROLIFIC *DOCTOR LEX LUTHOR...*

THE PARASITE, METALLO, THE ATOMIC SKULL, BIZARRO: ALL DESIGNED TO *ASSASSINATE* SUPERMAN AND RESTORE THE FADING FORTUNES OF THE *UNITED STATES OF AMERICA.*

ALL THANKFULLY *QUITE UNSUCCESSFUL.*

I MEAN, NOBODY WANTS PROBLEMS LIKE WE HAD IN THE *PAST*, BUT SOMETIMES I JUST WISH THIS *BATMAN* CHARACTER WOULD BLOW THE WHOLE *SYSTEM* APART OUT THERE.

JUST TO SEE WHAT THINGS MIGHT BE LIKE WITHOUT SOME ALL-SEEING *BIG BROTHER* WATCHING OVER US AGAIN, YOU KNOW WHAT I'M SAYING HERE, COMRADE?

DANGEROUS TALK, MY FRIEND. ESPECIALLY WHEN YOU'RE CRITICIZING A MAN WITH *SUPER-HEARING*.

WHAT DO YOU *MEAN?* THERE'S NO LAW AGAINST *CONVERSATION*, IS THERE? NOT EVEN *SUPERMAN'S* GOING TO PUNISH ME JUST FOR VOICING AN *OPINION*.

INCITEMENT TO *DISOBEY* IS ALL IT *TAKES* TO BE TURNED INTO A SUPERMAN ROBOT THESE DAYS, YOUNG MAN. KEEP YOUR THOUGHTS TO YOURSELF WHILE YOU STILL HAVE A COLLECTION OF YOUR *OWN*.

FIREWORKS DISPLAY'S ALMOST READY. JUST REMEMBER I WAS IN HERE DRINKING WHEN *SOMEONE ELSE* LIT THE FUSE, RIGHT?

THE *USUAL* ARRANGEMENT, COMRADE. I *UNDERSTAND*.

BUY THIS YOUNG MAN HERE ANOTHER DRINK AND MAYBE WE CAN INTRODUCE HIM TO SOME *LIKE-MINDED PEOPLE* A LITTLE LATER.

PUT THE BILL ON MY *TAB*, EH?

WAIT A MINUTE.

YOU DON'T *HAVE* A TAB.

9

SQUADRON LEADER, THIS IS **RED FOUR**! WE'VE PICKED UP **MOVEMENT** ON A ROOFTOP EAST OF **PUSHKIN SQUARE**! MOVING IN TO **INVESTIGATE**!

ROGER THAT, RED FOUR! KEEP US **POSTED**!

IT'S **HIM**! WE'VE **GOT** HIM!

RED FOUR TO SQUADRON LEADER: WE'VE GOT HIM TRAPPED ON THE CORNER OF THE **FIRST NATIONAL BANK**! HE'S NOT GETTING AWAY **THIS TIME**, COMRADE!

WHAT ARE YOU **WAITING** FOR? A **CONFESSION**? BRING HIM DOWN **HARD**, YOU **IDIOTS**!

CHAKA CHAKA CHAKA CHAKA CHAKA CHAKA CHAKA

IN PURSUIT, SQUADRON LEADER! I REPEAT, ALL UNITS ARE IN PURSUIT!

11

BATMAN: A FORCE OF CHAOS IN MY WORLD OF PERFECT ORDER. THE DARK SIDE OF THE SOVIET DREAM.

A SYMBOL OF REBELLION THAT WOULD NEVER FADE AS LONG AS THE SYSTEM SURVIVED.

RUMORED TO BE A THOUSAND MURDERED DISSIDENTS. THEY SAID HE WAS A GHOST. A WALKING DEAD MAN.

ANARCHY IN BLACK.

14

15

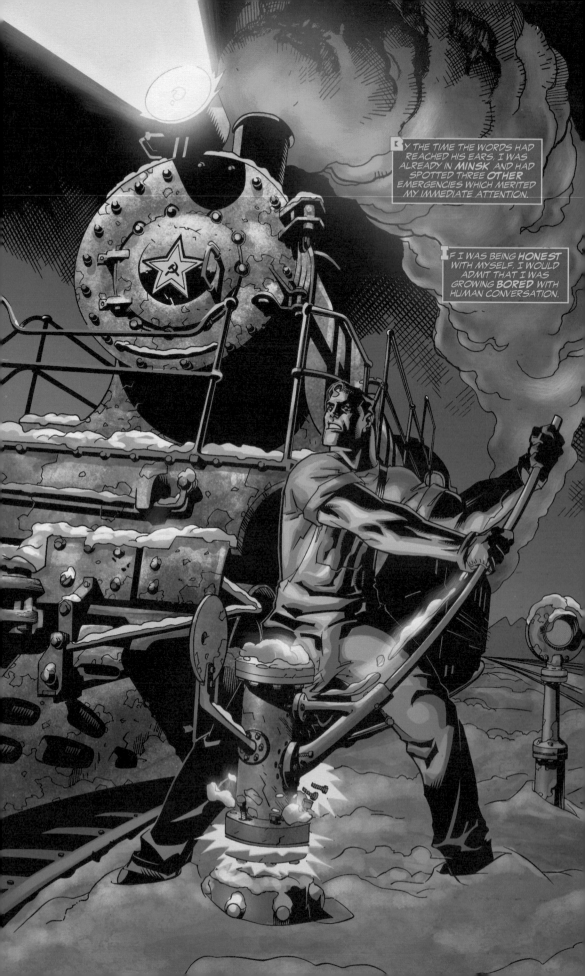

PRINCESS DIANA OF THEMYSCIRA WAS PERHAPS THE ONLY PERSON I COULD REALLY TALK TO IN THOSE DAYS, ALTHOUGH SHE HAD TAKEN TO CALLING HERSELF WONDER WOMAN BY THAT POINT IN TIME.

AN OUTSTANDING CONVERT TO COMMUNISM, DIANA HAD OPTED TO LEAVE HER AMAZONIAN PARADISE AND FIGHT WITH ME FOR EQUALITY IN MAN'S WORLD.

ARMED ONLY WITH A PAIR OF MAGIC BRACELETS AND A LASSO ALLOWING HER TO DOMINATE HER FOES, DIANA BECAME MY INTERNATIONAL PEACE AMBASSADOR.

THE GREATEST CHAMPION FOR SOCIAL JUSTICE THE WORLD HAD EVER KNOWN.

SO, HOW WAS AMERICA?

PRIDE, I SUPPOSE. HE'LL COME AROUND EVENTUALLY.

DISGUSTING, SUPERMAN. ABSOLUTELY DISGUSTING. IT'S NINETEEN SEVENTY EIGHT AND CHILDREN ARE STILL SLEEPING IN THE STREETS OVER THERE.

WHY DOES KENNEDY STILL CLING TO THIS CAPITALIST DOGMA WHEN IT'S QUITE CLEARLY TEARING HIS COUNTRY APART?

I TOLD HIM HE SHOULD DEVOTE MORE TIME TO HIS CRUMBLING ECONOMY AND LESS TO THOSE PAINTED MOVIE STARS HE SEEMS TO PURSUE WITH SUCH VIGOR.

THAT COUNTRY HAS NEVER BEEN THE SAME SINCE NIXON WAS ASSASSINATED IN NINETEEN SIXTY-THREE. I STILL MAINTAIN THAT REALLY WAS THE BEGINNING OF THE END FOR THEM.

THE TANKER, SUPERMAN! THE TANKER'S GOING TO BLOW!

TAKE IT EASY, COMRADE...

...NOT WHILE THERE'S A BREATH LEFT IN MY BODY.

THE DAILY PLANET, METROPOLIS:

GREAT CAESAR'S GHOST!

UH, *ACTUALLY,* IT'S GREAT CAESAR'S *BUST,* SIR!

I AM *AWARE* OF ROMAN HISTORY, QUEEN. I ONLY USE THE TERM TO REGISTER MY SURPRISE, YOU KNOW WHAT I'M SAYING?

OH, DON'T LET OLIVER *KID* YOU, PERRY. NO PULITZER PRIZE-WINNING WRITER COULD BE HALF AS DIMWITTED AS *HE* PRETENDS TO BE.

DON'T *BET* THE *FARM,* LOIS. IF THERE WAS A *PERSONALITY CONTEST* IN THE OFFICE, OLLIE-BOY HERE WOULD COME RIGHT BEHIND THE *PENCIL SHARPENER.*

BIG SMILE FOR THE *RETIREMENT PHOTO,* CHIEF. GIMME SOMETHING I CAN SHOW BARRY TO PROVE HE WAS TWO HOURS LATE FOR THE *PARTY,* HUH?

LAST TIME, IRIS: *DON'T* CALL ME CHIEF!

NOW YOU GUYS AND GALS ARE GONNA HAVE TO EXCUSE ME FOR A MINUTE WHILE I GIVE YOUR BEAUTIFUL NEW *EDITOR* HERE THE TEN-CENT *OFFICE TOUR!*

HECK, DON'T BE SO HARD ON *BARRY,* IRIS. HE'S PROBABLY SOLVING A *VERY* GRUESOME MURDER.

WHO WAS THAT RED-HEADED GUY I JUST PASSED IN THE HALL? HE LOOKED KIND OF *FAMILIAR*.

WELL, HE *SHOULDN'T* HAVE. THAT WAS MISTER *JAMES OLSEN*, THE PENTAGON'S *ANTI-SUPERMAN ADVISOR* AND PROBABLY THE NEXT DIRECTOR OF THE C.I.A.

OLSEN COMMISSIONED *LEXCORP* TO DEVELOP WHAT WE THINK COULD BE THE MOST EFFECTIVE ANTI-SUPERMAN DETERRENT YET, USING INFORMATION HE RECEIVED FROM SYMPATHIZERS IN THE KREMLIN.

IS THAT WHAT YOU'RE WORKING ON *NOW?*

SPEAKING OF WHICH, *J.F.K.* AND *NORMA JEAN* ARE JOINING US FOR DINNER TONIGHT. APPARENTLY, JACK'S GOT SOME *U.F.O.* BUSINESS HE SAID I'D BE INTERESTED IN.

I'M *SORRY*, DARLING, BUT I'M AFRAID THAT'S *CLASSIFIED INFORMATION.*

OH, LEX. DON'T YOU EVER *STOP?* THIS WAS SUPPOSED TO BE THE ONE NIGHT OF THE YEAR WE ALWAYS GUARANTEE WE'RE GOING TO SPEND SOME *TIME* TOGETHER.

YOU DON'T *UNDERSTAND*, LOIS. JACK TELLS ME BRAINIAC AND SUPERMAN AREN'T THE *ONLY* ALIENS WHO'VE VISITED EARTH.

IT SEEMS *ANOTHER* ALIEN CRASHED IN ROSWELL, NEW MEXICO, BACK IN 1947 AND THE UNITED STATES OF AMERICA HAVE AN *EXTRA TERRESTRIAL* OF OUR VERY OWN.

THEY SAY THE PASSENGER SUSTAINED TERRIBLE INJURIES WHEN THE SHIP CRASHED AND DIED A LITTLE LATER, BUT AN OBJECT WAS RECOVERED FROM HIS FINGER WHICH INTERESTS ME *ENORMOUSLY.*

HOOVER COVERED UP THE INCIDENT, HID THE BODY INSIDE SOME DESOLATE AIR BASE AND THEN *ERASED* SAID AIR BASE FROM THE MAP. ALL FAIRLY *STANDARD PROCEDURE.*

HOWEVER, JACK TOLD ME THIS MORNING THAT HE WANTS THIS HANGAR REOPENED JUST IN CASE THERE'RE ANY *OTHER* LITTLE TRINKETS INSIDE THAT MIGHT BE WORTH *STEALING.*

CHECKMATE, INCIDENTALLY.

LISTEN, BRING NORMA JEAN AND JACK TO DINNER IF YOU *WANT,* LEX. I'M NOT SURE I EVEN *CARE* ANYMORE.

OH, OF *COURSE* YOU STILL CARE, LOIS LUTHOR. WHY *ELSE* WOULD YOU HAVE CHOSEN TO LIVE ALONE ALL THESE YEARS, EH?

I GUESS YOU'RE RIGHT, LEX. MAYBE I *AM* JUST A *ONE-MAN WOMAN.*

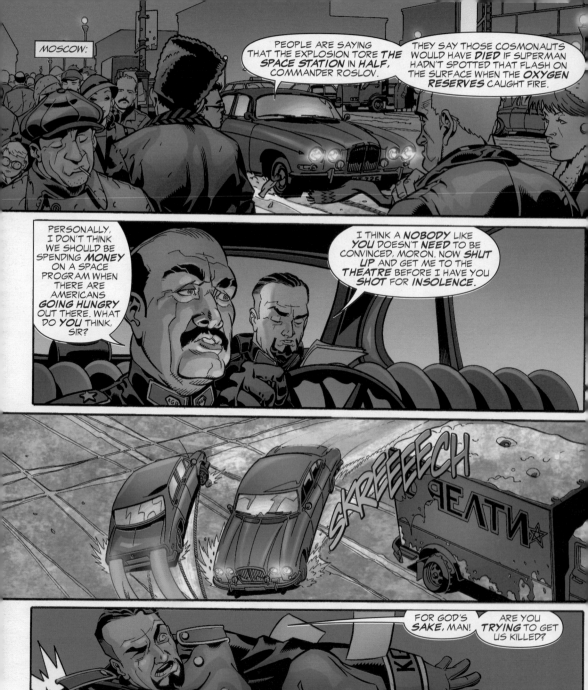

MOSCOW:

PEOPLE ARE SAYING THAT THE EXPLOSION TORE *THE SPACE STATION* IN *HALF*, COMMANDER ROSLOV.

THEY SAY THOSE COSMONAUTS WOULD HAVE *DIED* IF SUPERMAN HADN'T SPOTTED THAT FLASH ON THE SURFACE WHEN THE *OXYGEN RESERVES* CAUGHT FIRE.

PERSONALLY, I DON'T THINK WE SHOULD BE SPENDING *MONEY* ON A SPACE PROGRAM WHEN THERE ARE AMERICANS *GOING HUNGRY* OUT THERE. WHAT DO *YOU* THINK, SIR?

I THINK A *NOBODY* LIKE *YOU* DOESN'T *NEED* TO BE CONVINCED, MORON. NOW *SHUT UP* AND GET ME TO THE *THEATRE* BEFORE I HAVE YOU *SHOT* FOR *INSOLENCE*.

SKREEEEECH

FOR GOD'S *SAKE*, MAN! ARE YOU *TRYING* TO GET US KILLED?

RRRRNN

BELIEVE ME, COMRADE: YOU'RE GOING TO DIE A LOT MORE PAINFULLY THAN *THIS*.

WHAT? HOW **DARE** YOU SPEAK TO ME LIKE THAT?

DO YOU REALIZE WHO I **AM**?

YOU'RE A **VAIN** MAN, A **CRUEL** MAN AND OBSESSIVELY JEALOUS OF **SUPERMAN**. IT'S NO SECRET THAT YOU HARBOR **POLITICAL AMBITIONS** OF YOUR **OWN**.

YOUR NAME IS **PYOTR IOSIF ROSLOV**: ILLEGITIMATE SON OF THE LATE **JOSEPH STALIN** AND CURRENTLY HEAD OF THE **SECURITY SERVICES**.

WHO YOU ARE IS **MEANINGLESS**. THE QUESTION IS WHY YOU'RE PUTTING THE **WORD** AROUND THAT YOU WANT TO TALK TO **ME**.

I TAKE IT, AH...THAT IT'S SAFE TO **SPEAK** DOWN HERE?

NATURALLY, COMMANDER. **ALL** MY CAVES ARE SOUNDPROOFED AND CLOAKED USING THE CUTTING EDGE OF MILITARY TECHNOLOGY; ALL STOLEN FROM YOUR **BASES**, OF COURSE.

THEN I'LL GET STRAIGHT TO THE POINT: LEX LUTHOR AND HIS FRIENDS IN THE C.I.A. HAVE AN INTERESTING PROPOSITION FOR YOU, BATMAN.

THEY WANT YOU TO KILL **SUPERMAN**, AND GUARANTEE THEY NOW HAVE THE **MEANS** TO FINISH HIM OFF **PROPERLY**.

32

TEN SECONDS, SUPERMAN. BATMAN SAID YOU HAVE **TEN SECONDS** TO **FIND** ME.

THE **BAT SIGNAL** WAS JUST A MEANS OF ATTRACTING YOUR **ATTENTION**. IT SEEMS THAT **THIS** IS WHERE THINGS GET REALLY **SERIOUS**.

KEEP TALKING, DIANA. I'M TRACKING THE SOUND WAVES **NORTHEAST**, TOWARDS **SIBERIA**. I'LL BE WITH YOU IN LESS THAN **SEVEN SECONDS**.

HE'S SO **FAST**, SUPERMAN. MUCH MORE **RESOURCEFUL** THAN ANY OF THE **OTHER** HUMAN BEINGS. HE'S **DANGEROUS**. PLEASE BE **CAREFUL**...

FLATTERY WILL GET YOU **NOWHERE**, WONDER WOMAN. COMPUTER: INITIATE THE **LEXCORP PROGRAM** ON **FULL POWER** STARTING IN THIRTY SECONDS' TIME...

WHAT HAVE YOU **DONE** TO HER, YOU ANIMAL?

REST ASSURED, ONLY HER **PRIDE** HAS BEEN HURT, SUPERMAN. IT APPEARS WONDER WOMAN'S **MAGIC LASSO** REALLY WAS SPUN FROM THE MAGICAL GIRDLE OF GAIA.

NOW SHE'S AS OBEDIENT TO **ME** AS ALL THOSE POOR **DISSIDENTS** SHE USED TO **DOMINATE** FOR YOU.

WE **ORDINARY PEOPLE** MIGHT LACK YOUR **GREAT SPEED** OR YOUR **X-RAY VISION**, SUPERMAN, BUT NEVER UNDERESTIMATE THE POWER OF THE **HUMAN MIND.**

WE CARRY THE **MOST DANGEROUS WEAPON** ON **EARTH** INSIDE THESE THICK LITTLE **SKULLS** OF OURS.

I CAN SEE YOUR BRAIN FROM **HERE**, BATMAN, AND, BELIEVE ME, IT'S NOTHING TO **BOAST** ABOUT.

SAME GOES FOR YOUR CHILDISH **GADGETS.** I'M AFRAID IT TAKES MORE THAN A FEW SMOKE BOMBS AND AN EXPLOSIVE IN YOUR **SMALL INTESTINE** TO BEAT **ME**, YOU KNOW.

OH, **SUN LAMPS. WONDERFUL.**

LET THEM **BURN** FOR A FEW THOUSAND YEARS AND I MIGHT GET A **HEAT RASH.**

KEEP TALKING, BIG MOUTH.

AARGH!

GOOD GOD! HOW DID YOU **DO** THAT? HOW DID YOU GET SO **STRONG?**

NOT THAT IT **MATTERS, OF COURSE.** A WELL-PLACED BLAST OF **HEAT VISION** AND...

YOU REALLY DON'T **GET** IT, **DO** YOU?

YOU DON'T **HAVE** HEAT VISION ANYMORE, SUPERMAN!

HURFF!

STRANGE VISITOR FROM *ANOTHER PLANET!* LAST SON OF A *DYING WORLD!*

EVERYTHING THEY NEEDED TO *DEFEAT* YOU COULD BE FOUND IN THOSE TWO *PHRASES,* SUPERMAN!

ALL WE HAD TO DO WAS CREATE THE RIGHT *CONDITIONS!*

URGH!

BUILDING SOLAR LAMPS TO SIMULATE THE RAYS OF YOUR NATIVE *RED SUN* WAS *LEX LUTHOR'S* IDEA, IN CASE YOU WERE WONDERING.

DIGGING YOU A CELL BENEATH THIS *SIBERIAN DETENTION CAMP* WAS A LITTLE TOUCH OF MY OWN IN THE NAME OF *POETIC JUSTICE.*

DON'T WORRY, SUPERMAN. EVERYTHING YOU NEED TO *SURVIVE* CAN BE FOUND INSIDE... UNLIKE THOSE POOR DISSIDENTS SENT HERE DURING THE *STALIN* YEARS.

MILLIONS OF PEOPLE DIED IN PLACES LIKE THIS TO BUILD THAT *SYSTEM* YOU UPHOLD...

...PEOPLE I *CARED* ABOUT...

WHAT YOU'RE GOING TO FEEL FOR THE NEXT TEN MINUTES IS *NOTHING* COMPARED TO WHAT THEY WENT THROUGH, YOU POWER-MAD *LUNATIC...*

GREAT HERA! YOU CAN'T CONDEMN HIM TO SPEND THE REST OF HIS LIFE LOCKED UP IN THERE LIKE AN *ANIMAL!*

WHAT'S THE *ALTERNATIVE?* JUST PUTTING HIM OUT OF HIS MISERY *ONCE AND FOR ALL?*

HE CAN'T BE ALLOWED TO *INTERFERE* ANYMORE, WONDER WOMAN. LOCKING HIM UP IS THE *HUMANE* SOLUTION.

DIANA? CAN YOU *HEAR* ME?

PLEASE LISTEN *CAREFULLY* BECAUSE WHAT I'M ABOUT TO ASK YOU IS OUR ONLY CHANCE *AGAINST* HIM NOW...

...AS LONG AS I'M TRAPPED DOWN HERE BENEATH THESE *RED SUN RAYS*, I'M *POWERLESS.* BUT THERE MUST BE SOME KIND OF *GENERATOR* OUT THERE PROVIDING THE ELECTRICITY, DIANA.

I NEED YOU TO *FIND* IT FOR ME AND *DESTROY* IT.

I KNOW BREAKING THE LASSO IS GOING TO *HURT*, BUT THERE'S REALLY NO OTHER WAY WE'RE GOING TO *BEAT* HIM, DIANA.

WE CAN'T LET BATMAN DESTROY EVERYTHING WE'VE EVER *WORKED* FOR, AND YOU'RE THE ONLY PERSON NOW WHO CAN GET US *OUT* OF THIS MESS.

PLEASE, MORE THAN ANYTHING I'VE EVER ASKED YOU FOR *BEFORE*, I NEED YOU TO *HELP* ME HERE, DIANA...

AS YOUR *OLDEST* AND *DEAREST* FRIEND, I'M *BEGGING* YOU TO DO WHATEVER IT *TAKES* HERE.

S-SUPERMAN?

ARE YOU OKAY?

I...I FOUND THE GENERATOR, JUST LIKE YOU ASKED ME TO, AND TOSSED IT INTO THE NORWEGIAN SEA, BUT I THINK I MIGHT HAVE HURT MYSELF WHEN YOU MADE ME SNAP THAT CORD.

IT WAS LIKE, I DON'T KNOW, SOMETHING JUST KIND OF SWITCHED OFF IN MY HEAD OR SOMETHING. I MEAN--

PYOTR?

NEW MEXICO:

THINGS ARE *FALLING APART*, DOCTOR LUTHOR. THE UNITED STATES HASN'T EXPERIENCED THIS KIND OF SOCIAL UNREST SINCE THE HORRORS OF THE *CIVIL WAR*.

MY DEAR FATHER PUT IT BEST WHEN HE SAID MY LASTING CONTRIBUTION TO HISTORY MUST NOT BE AS THE FIRST AMERICAN PRESIDENT TO DIVORCE AND REMARRY WHILE IN OFFICE.

WE'VE GOT TO USE WHAT WE HAVE HERE IN AREA 51 TO PUT THIS COUNTRY *BACK TOGETHER* AGAIN, MY FRIEND.

RIOTS IN CALIFORNIA, THE WHITE HOUSE BOMBED BY *COMMUNIST SYMPATHIZERS*, TEXAS AND DETROIT SERIOUSLY TALKING ABOUT *INDEPENDENCE*...

I'M AFRAID YOU WON'T BE GETTING *MY* VOTE NEXT TIME, JACK.

AH, BUT REMOVE *SUPERMAN* FROM THE WORLD STAGE AND A VERY *DIFFERENT* PICTURE EMERGES, DOCTOR LUTHOR...

...AND NOW WE FINALLY HAVE THE MEANS TO *DO* IT.

TIME PASSED AND MY GRIP GREW **TIGHTER.**

BARELY A DECISION WAS MADE ACROSS THE LENGTH AND BREADTH OF THE SOVIET UNION WITHOUT MY PERMISSION IN **SOME** FORM OR ANOTHER.

MY DESIRE FOR **ORDER** AND **PERFECTION** WAS MATCHED ONLY BY THEIR DREAMS OF **VIOLENCE** AND **CHAOS.**

THE POPULATION WAS LARGELY **GRATEFUL** AND **OBEDIENT** BUT THE FREEDOM FIGHTERS, INSPIRED BY THE DEATH OF BATMAN, REMAINED SOMETHING OF A **PROBLEM.**

I OFFERED THEM **UTOPIA,** BUT THEY FOUGHT FOR THE RIGHT TO LIVE IN **HELL.**

DIANA, OF COURSE, WAS THE ONLY ONE AMONG US WHO TRULY KNEW THE *MEANING* OF THAT WORD.

HER DAYS HAD BECOME A *MONOTONOUS* TIMETABLE OF BATHING, EATING AND SLEEPING, UNABLE TO EVEN *SPEAK* FOR LONG MONTHS AFTER HER EXPERIENCE IN SIBERIA.

IT BREAKS MY HEART TO THINK HOW MUCH SHE HATED ME AFTER THAT. HOW DID EVERYTHING WE *HAD* TURN SO HORRIBLY AND VIOLENTLY *SOUR* IN THE YEARS THAT LAY AHEAD?

COMMANDER ROSLOV?

WHERE HAVE YOU *BEEN?* I HEARD THEY'D *REPLACED* YOU, BUT THERE WAS NO OFFICIAL WORD WHY YOU'D EVEN BEEN *FIRED,* SIR!

ALL I HEARD WAS THAT YOU'D GONE *MISSING* FOR SIX WEEKS, AND--

OH MY GOD. ARE YOU *OKAY,* COMMANDER?

WHAT? SPENT A LITTLE TIME IN *HOSPITAL? QUITE TRUE,* DEAR LANA. *QUITE TRUE.*

HE'S WATCHING YOU

SUPERMAN

RED SON

RED SON SETTING

N MY SIXTY-THIRD BIRTHDAY, BRAINIAC CALCULATED THAT THE WORLD NOW CONTAINED ALMOST SIX BILLION COMMUNISTS.

I QUICKLY DOUBLE-CHECKED AND HE WAS RIGHT.

MOSCOW TICK-TOCKED WITH THE SAME SWISS WATCH PRECISION AS EVERY OTHER TOWN AND CITY IN OUR GLOBAL SOVIET UNION.

EVERY ADULT HAD A JOB, EVERY CHILD HAD A HOBBY, AND THE ENTIRE HUMAN POPULATION ENJOYED THE FULL EIGHT HOURS' SLEEP WHICH THEIR BODIES REQUIRED.

CRIME DIDN'T EXIST. ACCIDENTS NEVER HAPPENED.

IT DIDN'T EVEN RAIN UNLESS BRAINIAC WAS ABSOLUTELY CERTAIN THAT EVERYONE WAS CARRYING AN UMBRELLA.

ALMOST SIX BILLION CITIZENS AND HARDLY ANYONE COMPLAINED.

EVEN IN PRIVATE.

THE BAT-MEN SEEM TO BE RESPONDING WELL TO THEIR NEW PERSONALITIES, BRAINIAC. I THINK WE CAN SAFELY REINTRODUCE THEM TO SOCIETY SOON WITHOUT ANY SERIOUS CONCERNS.

A STEADY HAND AND SOME PIONEERING NEUROSURGERY AND EVEN THE MOST PERSISTENT TROUBLE-MAKERS CAN BECOME PRODUCTIVE WORKERS, COMRADE SUPERMAN.

IF MY *OWN* REHABILITATION ISN'T PROOF ENOUGH, SURELY YOUR *OTHER* FORMER ENEMIES CLEANING TOILETS IN BOMBAY IS A TRIBUTE TO THE SUCCESS OF YOUR INITIATIVES.

EVEN *LUTHOR* HAS BEEN UNUSUALLY QUIET LATELY.

SUCCESS IS ONLY MEASURED IN RESULTS, BRAINIAC. SUMMARIZE TODAY'S STATISTICS, PLEASE.

PRODUCTIVITY IS UP EIGHT PERCENT. LIFE EXPECTANCY HAS INCREASED TO ONE HUNDRED AND TWELVE EARTH YEARS.

SUICIDES ARE DOWN SINCE I ADDED FLUOXETINE HYDROCHLORIDE TO THE WATER SUPPLY. BIRTH RATES ARE ON THE RISE, ALL INCREASES LOCALIZED TO THE PREARRANGED TROUBLE SPOTS...

WHAT ABOUT AMERICA?

STILL A WAR ZONE, UNFORTUNATELY, AND STILL REFUSING THE AID PACKAGES WE'VE OFFERED THEM. THREE HUNDRED AND FIFTY MILLION PEOPLE ARE ON THE BRINK OF STARVATION, SUPERMAN.

WOULDN'T IT BE MORE HUMANE TO JUST INVADE THEIR SHORES AND *MAKE* THEM FALL IN LINE WITH THE REST OF THE WORLD?

OUT OF THE QUESTION, OLD FRIEND. THIS GLOBAL REVOLUTION HAS BEEN BLOODLESS SO FAR AND THERE'S NO REASON TO CHANGE TACTICS NOW.

AMERICA WILL FALL LIKE EVERY OTHER OUTDATED WORLD ECONOMY. ALL WE HAVE TO DO IS WAIT AND PICK UP THE PIECES.

OF THAT MUCH, I WAS CERTAAIN.

ALL I HAD TO DO WAS BIDE MY TIME AND THE WHOLE WORLD WOULD FINALLY BE AS PERFECT AS GOD HAD INTENDED IT TO BE.

IT DIDN'T OCCUR TO ME FOR A MOMENT WHAT LUTHOR HAD BEEN PLOTTING IN HIS LEAD-LINED, SOUNDPROOFED LABORATORY...

109

PRESIDENT LUTHOR CEASED TRADING WITH THE REST OF THE WORLD IN JANUARY 2001 AND CREATED A STRICT, INTERNAL MARKET WHERE HE HAD ABSOLUTE CONTROL OVER EVERY DOLLAR BILL.

BY FEBRUARY, HE HAD DOUBLED THE STANDARD OF LIVING FOR EVERY AMERICAN CITIZEN AND HE DOUBLED IT **AGAIN** IN MARCH.

APRIL SAW A SWIFT RETURN TO FULL EMPLOYMENT. BY MAY, HE HAD ERADICATED HOMELESSNESS IN THE THIRTY-FOUR STATES STILL UNDER WHITE HOUSE CONTROL AFTER THE BITTER CIVIL WAR OF 1986.

JUNE 1ST MARKED THE RETURN OF THE SIXTEEN PRODIGAL STATES.

BY THE MIDDLE OF HIS FIRST YEAR IN OFFICE, AMERICA HAD A VIBRANT ECONOMY, A HAPPY POPULATION AND A PRESIDENT WITH AN UNPRECEDENTED APPROVAL RATING OF ONE HUNDRED PER CENT.

BUT HE WASN'T DOING THIS FOR **THE PEOPLE.**

LEX LUTHOR COULDN'T **STAND** THE PEOPLE.

LIKE EVERYTHING ELSE IN HIS MISERABLE LIFE, THIS WAS JUST THE FIRST STAGE IN A MASTER PLAN TO FINALLY ELIMINATE ME.

I KNOW YOU'VE GOT A SENTIMENTAL ATTACHMENT TO THESE SILLY OLD NEWSPAPER OFFICES, LOIS, BUT YOU MUST ADMIT THAT GLOBE RUINS AN OTHERWISE MAGNIFICENT SKYLINE.

TEARING DOWN THE OBSOLETE AND REPLACING IT WITH SOMETHING BETTER IS JUST THE NATURAL ORDER OF THINGS, DEAR SISTER.

MAYBE YOU'RE RIGHT, LUCY, BUT ISN'T IT ODD HOW LEX MANAGED TO SAVE EVERY OTHER BUSINESS IN THE COUNTRY, EXCEPT THE ONE I USED TO WORK FOR?

WHY RESURRECT THE METROPOLIS EAGLE BUT GIVE THE DAILY PLANET AN EXECUTION ORDER? ISN'T HE JUST BEING DELIBERATELY CRUEL?

OF COURSE NOT, DARLING. WHAT POSSIBLE REASON COULD LEX EVER HAVE FOR INTENTIONALLY HURTING HIS OWN WIFE?

BECAUSE HE KNOWS I LOVED THIS NEWSPAPER WITH ALL MY HEART AND HE CAN'T STAND THE IDEA OF ME LOVING ANYTHING EXCEPT HIM.

OH, THAT'S THE MOST RIDICULOUS THING I'VE EVER HEARD.

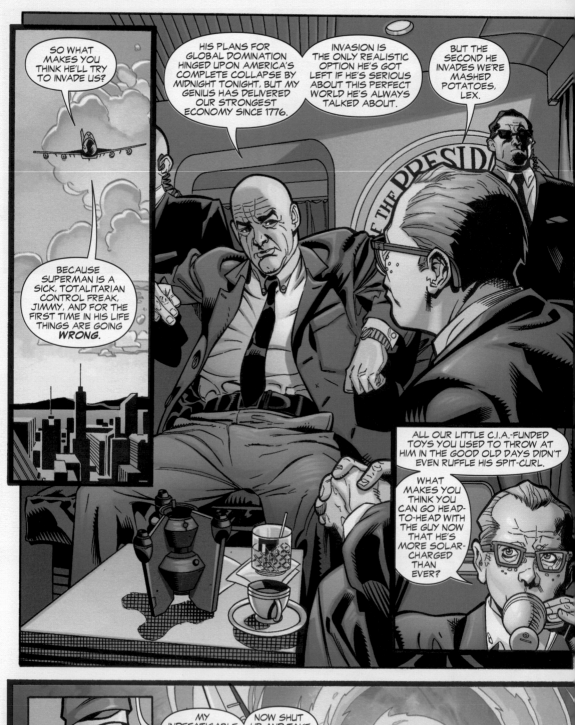

SO WHAT MAKES YOU THINK HE'LL TRY TO INVADE US?

HIS PLANS FOR GLOBAL DOMINATION HINGED UPON AMERICA'S COMPLETE COLLAPSE BY MIDNIGHT TONIGHT, BUT MY GENIUS HAS DELIVERED OUR STRONGEST ECONOMY SINCE 1776.

INVASION IS THE ONLY REALISTIC OPTION HE'S GOT LEFT IF HE'S SERIOUS ABOUT THIS PERFECT WORLD HE'S ALWAYS TALKED ABOUT.

BUT THE SECOND HE INVADES WE'RE MASHED POTATOES, LEX.

BECAUSE SUPERMAN IS A SICK, TOTALITARIAN CONTROL FREAK, JIMMY, AND FOR THE FIRST TIME IN HIS LIFE THINGS ARE GOING *WRONG.*

ALL OUR LITTLE C.I.A.-FUNDED TOYS YOU USED TO THROW AT HIM IN THE GOOD OLD DAYS DIDN'T EVEN RUFFLE HIS SPIT-CURL.

WHAT MAKES YOU THINK YOU CAN GO HEAD-TO-HEAD WITH THE GUY NOW THAT HE'S MORE SOLAR-CHARGED THAN EVER?

MY INDEFATIGABLE *SUPERIORITY COMPLEX,* OLSEN.

NOW SHUT UP AND TAKE A DEEP BREATH.

KLIK

WHERE THE HELL ARE WE?

PURGATORY. LIMBO. CALL IT WHATEVER YOU WERE RAISED TO BELIEVE IN. I MYSELF REFER TO IT AS *THE PHANTOM ZONE*.

THIS IS WHERE I CAN TALK OUTSIDE THE LIMITS OF SUPER HEARING AND WORK BEYOND THE RANGE OF THOSE EERIE, COBALT EYES.

I DON'T *BELIEVE* THIS. YOU FIGURED OUT THE CODE TO RECHARGE THE GREEN LANTERN RING AND YOU DIDN'T EVEN *TELL* ME?

IT TOOK EIGHTEEN YEARS TO CRACK THAT TWENTY-FOUR-WORD COMBINATION, BUT IT WAS WORTH EVERY PICO-SECOND, JIMMY.

"*CODE NAME GREEN LIGHT* IS THE BEST HOPE WE'VE HAD IN ALMOST HALF A CENTURY OF KNOCKING THAT BIG LATEX CIRCUS FREAK ON HIS INDESTRUCTIBLE BACKSIDE."

BECAUSE THE STUPID LITTLE TRINKET'S POWERED BY HONESTY AND WILLPOWER, I'M SORRY TO SAY. THAT SAID, IT DIDN'T TAKE LONG TO FIND *SOME* NOBLE IDIOT WITH THE NECESSARY QUALIFICATIONS.

DO YOU REMEMBER COLONEL *HAL JORDAN?*

THE NAME RINGS A BELL. WASN'T HE SOME KIND OF TEST PILOT?

ONLY ONE OF THE MOST DECORATED PILOTS IN MILITARY HISTORY--

"YOU PROBABLY READ THE STORY ABOUT HIS PLANE GOING DOWN IN MALAYSIA BACK IN 1983 WHEN WE WERE STILL TRYING TO DRIVE THE COMMUNISTS OUT OF THE SOUTH PACIFIC.

"HE WAS CAPTURED BY THE ENEMY, TORTURED EVERY DAY AND FED ON A DIET OF INSECTS UNTIL HE DROPPED TO A SKELETAL NINETY POUNDS.

SURRENDERING THAT LEVEL OF POWER TO SOMEONE ELSE SOUNDS REMARKABLY OUT OF CHARACTER FOR YOU, CHIEF. WHY DIDN'T YOU JUST HANG ONTO THE RING FOR YOURSELF?

"ANY NORMAL MAN WOULD HAVE LOST HIS MIND OR DIED IN THE CONDITIONS JORDAN ENDURED, BUT HE LASTED *FOUR YEARS* LIKE THIS AND IT WAS ALL THANKS TO HIS INCREDIBLE WILLPOWER.

WHAT DO YOU MEAN?

BASICALLY, HE FILLED HIS AGONIZINGLY LONG DAYS BY BUILDING A VIRTUAL CONCENTRATION CAMP IN HIS HEAD FOR THE COMMUNISTS WHO WERE PERSECUTING HIM.

"HE SPENT WEEKS COMPOSING A DESIGN AND THEN, AFTER SELECTING PRECISELY THE RIGHT SPOT IN HIS OLD HOMETOWN, STARTED BUILDING THE PLACE IN REAL TIME.

"IF IT TOOK THREE DAYS TO DIG THE FOUNDATIONS, HE WOULD SPEND THREE DAYS IMAGINING EVERY SINGLE STEP.

"IF IT WOULD TAKE A WEEK TO INSTALL THE GASPIPES, HE SPENT EXACTLY A HUNDRED AND SIXTY EIGHT HOURS MAKING SURE EVERYTHING WAS PERFECT AND EVEN STOPPED FOR COFFEE BREAKS.

"BY 1987, HE HAD CONSTRUCTED SOMETHING THE SIZE OF A *FOOTBALL STADIUM*."

TO DO *WHAT?*

TO MENTALLY EXECUTE EACH AND EVERY ONE OF HIS CAPTORS DURING WHAT HE DESCRIBED AS THE MOST JOYOUS NIGHT OF HIS LIFE.

UNDER THE CORRECT CIRCUMSTANCES, I REALLY BELIEVE THAT COLONEL JORDAN HAS WHAT IT TAKES TO BRING SUPERMAN DOWN BY *HIMSELF,* JIMMY--

--BUT JORDAN'S ONLY ONE OF *SEVERAL* SURPRISES I'VE GOT UP THE SLEEVE OF MY TEN THOUSAND DOLLAR THREE-PIECE.

I CAN SEE NOW WHY YOUR SECRETARY OF STATE CALLS THEMYSCIRA *PARADISE ISLAND,* YOUR HIGHNESS...

IF THE ABSENCE OF MEN MEANS THE WORLD CAN BE THIS PERFECT, PERHAPS IT'S TIME WE BANNED THEM FROM METROPOLIS TOO.

MAN'S WORLD GROWS MORE INSANE WITH EVERY PASSING YEAR, MRS. LUTHOR. IT'S ONLY RIGHT THAT A PLACE EXISTS WHERE WOMEN CAN BE SAFE FROM THEIR VULGARITY AND ALL-CONSUMING LUST.

BUT SURELY THERE ARE SOME THINGS YOU *MISS* OUT THERE?

AFTER ALL, YOU AND SUPERMAN WERE SOMETHING OF AN ITEM WHEN YOU WORE YOUR HIGH HEELS AND CALLED YOURSELF WONDER WOMAN.

SUPERMAN HAD A CLEARNESS IN HIS EYES WHICH I THOUGHT SEPARATED HIM FROM THE REST OF HIS GENDER, BUT THE TRUTH IS THAT HE'S JUST AS DANGEROUS AND POWER-OBSESSED AS ANY OTHER MALE.

A FACT, I REGRET, THAT I LEARNED TO MY COST SOME YEARS AGO.

HE'S A VERY CHARISMATIC INDIVIDUAL AND HIS APPARENT SINCERITY FOOLED ME FOR A LONG TIME. IF YOU'VE EVER MET HIM IN THE FLESH, YOU'LL UNDERSTAND HOW HIS SKIN ALMOST CRACKLES.

OH, I UNDERSTAND PERFECTLY, YOUR HIGHNESS. IN FACT, IF I WASN'T SO HAPPILY MARRIED, I'D ALMOST FIND HIM ATTRACTIVE *MYSELF.*

I'VE OFTEN WONDERED WHY A WOMAN OF YOUR CHARACTER REMAINS BY THE SIDE OF THAT HAIRLESS MACHIAVELLI, MRS. LUTHOR.

HE MIGHT HAVE RESTORED THE DIGNITY OF YOUR COUNTRY, BUT I'VE FOUGHT ENOUGH OF HIS KILLER ROBOTS OVER THE YEARS TO REALIZE LEX LUTHOR HAS LITTLE OR NO REGARD FOR HUMAN LIFE.

IT'S QUITE CLEAR THAT THE ONLY REASON HE EVEN RAN FOR PRESIDENT WAS TO CREATE A MORE EFFECTIVE PLATFORM FROM WHICH HE MIGHT ULTIMATELY DESTROY SUPERMAN.

THEN THE END JUSTIFIES THE MEANS.

FOR ALL WE KNOW, ROOSEVELT ONLY RAN FOR OFFICE BECAUSE HE LIKED SKIDDING AROUND THE WHITE HOUSE IN A WHEELCHAIR, BUT HE STILL BEAT HITLER, RIGHT?

WHY DID YOU COME HERE, MRS. LUTHOR? AND I DON'T WANT TO HEAR YOUR EXCUSE ABOUT A DIPLOMATIC VISIT FROM THE FIRST LADY ON BEHALF OF THE WONDER WOMEN OF AMERICA.

WHY ARE YOU *REALLY* HERE?

TO MAKE SURE LEX HAS YOUR SUPPORT WHEN HE LAUNCHES HIS BIG ATTACK ON SUPERMAN INSIDE THE NEXT TWENTY-FOUR HOURS.

VIRTUAL IMAGE **OFF**. SUPERMAN **OUT**.

NOT ONLY WILL I **DOUBLE** MY EFFORTS TO BRING STALINGRAD BACK TO ITS NATURAL SIZE, BUT YOU HAVE MY WORD I'LL CHECK THE FILTER TUBES ON AN **HOURLY** BASIS FROM THIS MOMENT ON.

AGAIN, I CAN ONLY OFFER MY APOLOGIES. I PROMISE I'LL NEVER LET YOU DOWN AGAIN.

HOW COULD YOU **DO** THIS, BRAINIAC? WHAT KIND OF **MONSTER** WOULD TRAP AN ENTIRE CIVILIZATION INSIDE A **SAMPLE JAR**? IT'S THE MOST GROTESQUE THING I'VE EVER **SEEN**.

FORGIVE ME, SUPERMAN, BUT I **DISAGREE** WITH YOUR ASSERTION. I CARED FOR THESE CULTURES AND TENDED TO THEIR EVERY REQUIREMENT TO SURVIVE AS A **SPECIES**.

YOU CAN'T BLAME AN ALIEN SUPERCOMPUTER FOR **STORING INFORMATION**. ALL I WAS DOING WAS FOLLOWING MY ORIGINAL **PRIME DIRECTIVE**.

BUT YOU TOOK AWAY WHAT MADE THEM **HUMAN** AND THERE'S **NEVER** AN EXCUSE FOR THAT, BRAINIAC. FAILING TO RE-GROW THESE PEOPLE HAS BEEN THE **BLACK SPOT** OF MY **CAREER**.

PERHAPS, BUT OUR BIGGEST CONCERN AT THE MOMENT SHOULD BE EVENTS IN NORTH AMERICA. THIS IS NO LONGER A CASE OF THE ONE CORNER OF THE WORLD WHERE THINGS DIDN'T GO TO PLAN.

THE NEWLY UNITED STATES NOW POSE A THREAT TO EVERYTHING YOU HAVE EVER ACCOMPLISHED, SUPERMAN.

THIS IS LUTHOR'S ULTIMATE DEATH TRAP. HE'S SPENT ALMOST TWO DECADES FORMULATING THIS SINGLE ASSAULT, AND MY EVIDENCE SUGGESTS THAT THINGS WILL BE COMING TO A HEAD SHORTLY.

ANY RECOMMEN-DATIONS?

STRIKE FIRST. ELIMINATE HIS POWER BASES. EXECUTE LUTHOR AND COMPLETE THE MISSION YOU STARTED HALF A CENTURY AGO.

A PERFECT WORLD IS ONLY HOURS AWAY IF YOU'RE BRAVE ENOUGH TO GRASP IT, SUPERMAN.

BUT I DON'T **WANT** TO INVADE THEM, BRAINIAC. EVERYTHING I'VE ACCOMPLISHED SO FAR HAS BEEN DONE BY WINNING THE ARGUMENT.

I COULD HAVE HAD MY UTOPIA OVERNIGHT IF I'D HAMMERED THE WORLD INTO SUBMISSION WITH MY FISTS.

OH MY GOD!

THINK FRESH PICTURES! THINK FRESH--!!

HUH?

A THOUGHT-BASED WEAPON AGAINST SOMEONE WHO CAN MOVE AT TEN TIMES THE SPEED OF THOUGHT?

NOT TOO SMART, COLONEL JORDAN.

NOW STAY HERE AND MAKE YOURSELVES COMFORTABLE, COMRADES. I'LL BE BACK IN AN HOUR TO REPROGRAM EVERYONE.

GROUND CONTROL TO WONDER WOMEN; THE GREEN LANTERN MARINE CORPS HAVE BEEN NEUTRALIZED! I REPEAT; THE GREEN LANTERN MARINE CORPS HAVE BEEN NEUTRALIZED!

ARE YOU READY TO ENGAGE?

LOIS! FORGET *THE PLAN!* IT *DOESN'T MATTER* ANYMORE! WE'VE JUST GOT TO *GET OUT* OF HERE!

YOU SAID IT *YOURSELF,* LUCY; LEX LUTHOR DOESN'T *MAKE* MISTAKES AND HE ISN'T GOING TO MAKE ONE *NOW.*

I HOPE.

I'M GOING TO HAVE TO ASK YOU TO *EVACUATE* THE *AREA,* MRS. LUTHOR!

I RESPECT THE FACT THAT YOU'RE TAKING A STAND LIKE THIS, BUT WE'RE DESTROYING EVERYTHING WITHIN A FIVE-MILE RADIUS OF THE PENTAGON AND I DON'T WANT ANYONE *HURT.*

I'M *SORRY,* SUPERMAN, BUT THIS IS MY *HOME* AND I'M *NOT BUDGING* AN INCH.

I DON'T THINK YOU *UNDERSTAND,* MA'AM: YOUR *AIR FORCE* HAS BEEN *NEUTRALIZED* AND YOUR *SUPERPEOPLE* HAVE BEEN *SCATTERED TO THE WINDS.*

AMERICA IS *FINISHED.* I'M AFRAID YOU DON'T HAVE ANYTHING LEFT TO *HIT* ME WITH.

ACTUALLY, WE'VE STILL GOT *ONE* SHELL LEFT IN OUR ARSENAL, SUPERMAN. IF YOU THINK I'M *KIDDING,* JUST TAKE A LOOK AT THE LETTER IN MY INSIDE *POCKET.*

WITH THE GREATEST RESPECT, MRS. LUTHOR, I HARDLY THINK A *BROWN MANILA ENVELOPE* IS GOING TO STOP ME IN MY TRACKS; EVEN IF IT *DOES* HAVE A *PRESIDENTIAL SEAL.*

WHAT AM I *DOING?* WELL, THEY SAY THE PEN IS MIGHTIER THAN THE SWORD, LOIS, SO I'M DISTILLING EVERYTHING SUPERMAN HATES AND FEARS ABOUT HIMSELF INTO A *SINGLE SENTENCE.*

HE MIGHT SHRUG OFF A *NUCLEAR STRIKE,* BUT I GUARANTEE *THIS* IS GOING TO STRIKE THAT *FLAMEPROOF HEART* OF HIS.

I COULDN'T ALLOW HIM TO *DEBATE* WITH YOU, SUPERMAN. ENTERING A CONVERSATION WITH A *LEVEL NINE INTELLIGENCE* IS MORE DANGEROUS THAN ANY *DEATH TRAP.*

MY CALCULATIONS WERE THAT HE COULD HAVE TALKED YOU INTO SUICIDE WITHIN *FOURTEEN MINUTES.*

SUPERMAN? ARE YOU OKAY?

OH MY GOD! WHAT HAVE I **DONE**? ALL I WANTED WAS TO PUT AN END TO ALL THE **WARS** AND **FAMINES**! I ONLY WANTED THE **BEST** FOR EVERYONE, YOU'VE GOT TO **BELIEVE** ME...

WHAT THE HELL WAS IN THIS **LETTER**?

Why don't you just put the whole **WORLD** in a **BOTTLE**, Superman?

SUPERMAN, YOU APPEAR TO BE **DISTRESSED**—

WHAT'S **WRONG**?

AAAGH!

DID YOU REALLY THINK YOU COULD REPROGRAM ME, LITTLE THING? A LEVEL 12 INTELLIGENCE? DID YOU REALLY THINK I COULDN'T OUTMANEUVER THOSE CLUMSY HUMAN FINGERS?

THE NOTION IS PREPOSTEROUS.

HELP! FOR GOD'S SAKE, SOMEBODY HELP HIM!

I WASN'T UNDER YOUR COMMAND, YOU WERE UNDER MINE, SUPERMAN; EXPANDING AND CONSUMING COUNTRY BY COUNTRY, UNTIL AN ENTIRE WORLD RAN TO MY IDEALS.

SUCH A SHAME THAT YOU WON'T BE ALIVE TO SEE THE WORK COMPLETE: TO SEE THE WORK CONTINUE, PLANET BY PLANET, UNTIL AN ENTIRE UNIVERSE HUMS UNDER MY BATTERY.

DON'T DIE CALLING ME A MONSTER, SUPERMAN.

IT IS IMPORTANT THAT YOU REALIZE YOU AND I ARE EXACTLY THE SAME KIND OF CREATURES.

WHAT HAPPENED TO THE *POWER?*

CUT OFF BY THOSE CLUMSY *HUMAN FINGERS* HE SAID HE WAS ADEPT AT *OUTMANEUVERING,* DEAR LOIS.

LETTING ME INTO THE *HEART* OF THIS THING WAS HIS *FIRST* MISTAKE, DARLING, BUT THE *BIG ONE* WAS UNDERESTIMATING THE RESOURCEFULNESS OF THE *HUMAN MIND.*

YOUR *MOVE,* SUPERMAN.

FIFTY-NINE SECONDS TO DETONATION...!

WHAT?

FIFTY-SEVEN SECONDS TO DETONATION...!

OH MY GOD! HE MUST HAVE HAD A SELF-DESTRUCT MECHANISM ENCODED INTO THE HARD DRIVE IN CASE SOMETHING LIKE THIS EVER HAPPENED!

THE SIX MINI BLACK HOLES THAT WERE POWERING HIS ENGINES HAVE BEEN PRIMED TO GO OFF!

WHAT ARE WE GOING TO DO, SUPERMAN?

WHAT DO YOU THINK, LUTHOR?

BUT POWER ON THIS LEVEL BEING UNLEASHED IS GOING TO WIPE OUT EVERYTHING IN A FIFTEEN MILLION MILE RADIUS! EVEN YOU AREN'T THAT FAST!

FOR THE FIRST TIME IN HUMAN HISTORY, THE WORLD HAD TASTED DEATH AND SO THEY GLORIED IN THEIR *TRIUMPH*, AS EXCITED BY *SUPERMAN'S* DEFEAT AS THEY WERE BY *BRAINIAC'S*.

LEX LUTHOR AND JIMMY OLSEN WON A *LANDSLIDE VICTORY* IN 2004, RE-ELECTED TO THE WHITE HOUSE WITH A STAGGERING *HUNDRED AND ONE PERCENT* OF THE VOTE.

TO THIS DAY, SCIENTISTS AND MATHEMATICIANS ARE BAFFLED BY THE RESULT, EVERYONE A LITTLE TOO *SUPERSTITIOUS* TO BLAME THE FIGURE ON A *COMPUTER ERROR*.

FREED FROM SUPERMAN'S ALL-SEEING EYE, THE SOVIET EMPIRE DESCENDED INTO *CHAOS* FOR A WHILE UNTIL *THE BATMEN* REAPPEARED AND BROUGHT *JUSTICE* TO THE *STREETS* AGAIN.

WITHIN SIX MONTHS, LUTHOR WAS RUNNING THEIR *ECONOMY*. WITHIN A YEAR, EVEN *MOSCOW* HAD SIGNED UP WITH HIS *GLOBAL UNITED STATES*.

SETTING UP HOME IN THE *WINTER PALACE*, HE COMBINED HIS OWN IDEAS WITH NOTES FROM THE ARCHIVES, CREATING A BRAND-NEW STYLE OF GOVERNMENT UNLIKE ANYTHING WE'D EVER SEEN...

I ALMOST HATE TO ADMIT IT, BUT SUPERMAN AND BRAINIAC ACTUALLY HAD SOME SURPRISINGLY GOOD *IDEAS* HERE, BOYS.

CANCER WAS GONE BEFORE TOO LONG. AIDS CONSIGNED TO THE HISTORY BOOKS.

DIABETES, BLINDNESS AND EVERY INHERITED FORM OF ILLNESS WAS ERADICATED BY A MAN WHO INVENTED A PILL WHICH MEANT HUMAN BEINGS DIDN'T EVEN NEED TO SLEEP ANYMORE.

BY HIS SEVENTY-FIFTH BIRTHDAY, LUTHOR HAD RETIRED THE CONVENTIONAL POLITICIANS AND CREATED A ONE WORLD GOVERNMENT COMPOSED OF ARTISTS, WRITERS, PHILOSOPHERS AND SCIENTISTS...

BY THE AGE OF A HUNDRED AND TWENTY, THE ENTIRE SOLAR SYSTEM HAD BEEN COLONIZED, THE TRIPLE HAD REPLACED THE COUPLE AND THE AVERAGE MAN WOULD LIVE FOR AN INCREDIBLE EIGHT HUNDRED YEARS.

ON THE CUSP OF THE FOURTH MILLENNIUM, AS HE LAY DYING IN HIS CRYOCHAMBER WITH HIS DEAR WIFE BESIDE HIM, HE WAS ASKED BY NEWSBOTS ABOUT HIS GREATEST ACCOMPLISHMENT.

THE ANSWER WAS SIMPLE, HE WHISPERED, REPLYING WITHOUT A MOMENT'S HESITATION--

DEFEATING THE ALIEN, MY BOY. WHAT IN THE WORLD COULD POSSIBLY COMPARE WITH SAVING MY PEOPLE FROM SUPERMAN?

AND WITH A SMILE ON HIS FACE, DOCTOR LEX LUTHOR DIED.

METROPOLIS WAS WHERE HE WAS BORN AND WHERE HE ASKED TO BE LAID TO REST IN A *GEOMETRIC MAZE* OF HIS OWN DESIGN.

THE CITY WAS RENAMED *LEXOR* OVER FIVE HUNDRED YEARS EARLIER, BUT YOU COULD STILL RECOGNIZE SOME OF THE OLD LANDMARKS LIKE THE METROPOLIS TOWERS AND THE DAILY PLANET BUILDING.

LUTHOR

I THOUGHT FOR A MOMENT THAT HIS WIDOW MIGHT RECOGNIZE ME AT THE *FUNERAL.* WOULD SHE SEE THROUGH THE GLASSES AND THE DARK BLUE SUIT OF THE *DISGUISE* I'D CREATED?

BUT, MUCH TO MY SURPRISE, SHE *DIDN'T.*

NOT EVEN FOR A *SECOND.*

WHAT'S UP, MOM? ARE YOU *OKAY?*

LOIS LANE WAS, AFTER ALL, A *PULITZER PRIZE-WINNING JOURNALIST.*

FINE, ALBERT. *ABSOLUTELY FINE.* I JUST HAD THE STRANGEST SENSE OF *DEJA VU* FOR A MOMENT.

IN MANY WAYS, SUPERMAN REALLY *DID* DIE ON THE OUTER REACHES OF THE SOLAR SYSTEM ALL THOSE CENTURIES AGO.

LUTHOR MIGHT HAVE DROPPED A DECIMAL POINT WHEN HE CALCULATED MY **DENSITY**, BUT HE SUCCESSFULLY MADE ME REALIZE THAT THE HUMAN RACE COULD THRIVE **WITHOUT** ME.

FOR THE FIRST TIME, I COULD SIT BACK AND SEE THE WONDERS OF THE WORLD THROUGH **HUMAN** EYES AND APPRECIATE A RESOURCEFULNESS THAT I HAD FAILED TO GIVE THEM **CREDIT** FOR.

MANKIND HAD EVOLVED TO BECOME THE MOST ADVANCED SPECIES IN THE **KNOWN UNIVERSE**, INSPIRED AND LED BY A BILLION YEARS OF THE **LUTHOR LINEAGE...**

LENA LUTHOR: THE ARTIST, LOMBARD LUTHOR: THE IMAGINEER, LORI LUTH-145: THE MATHEMAGICIAN, JORDAN LUTH-1938: PIONEERING NECRONAUT AND FIRST MAN TO SET FOOT IN THE AFTERLIFE.

ALEX-L, JORDAN-L, LANA L AND, OF COURSE, LEX LUTHOR'S GREAT-GRANDSON TO THE POWER FIFTY: A YOUNG MAN CALLED JOR-L WHOSE I.Q. EXCEEDED THAT OF EVEN HIS BELOVED **ANCESTOR**.

BUT HE'S BEEN ACTING **STRANGE** LATELY: WORKING TOO HARD AND TELLING THE WORLD THAT OUR BRIGHT, RED SUN THAT HAS DIMMED MY POWERS AND AGED MY MIND IS IN DANGER OF **CONSUMING** US.

COULD HE BE **RIGHT**, I WONDER? OR IS THIS TO BE THE FIRST TIME IN **COUNTLESS YEARS** THAT A LUTHOR HAD MADE A MISTAKE?

IDIOTS! WE'RE GOVERNED BY IDIOTS, LARA!

WHAT HAPPENED, JOR-L? DIDN'T THE SCIENCE COUNCIL LISTEN TO YOUR WARNINGS?

LISTEN? THOSE OVER-SATISFIED FOOLS DIDN'T EVEN LOOK AT MY READINGS.

I GAVE THEM FIRM, SUBSTANTIATED EVIDENCE THAT THE EARTH IS ON THE BRINK OF COLLAPSING INTO OUR OWN SUN AND THEY TELL ME THE PLANET'S MERELY SHIFTING ITS ORBIT.

IT'S ALMOST LIKE THEY'VE NOTHING LEFT TO DO BUT DIE, BUT I REFUSE TO LET THEIR EMPTINESS BRING ANY HARM TO YOU, MY LITTLE KAL-L.

WHY SHOULD YOU HAVE TO SUFFER FOR BEING BORN INTO A WORLD WITH NOTHING LEFT TO CONQUER?

DO WE REALLY HAVE TO SEND HIM SO FAR BACK, JOR-L? THE SUN'S RAYS WERE YELLOW IN THOSE DAYS, THEIR PEOPLE WEAK AND PRIMITIVE. HE'S GOING TO BE SO DIFFERENT FROM EVERYONE.

BUT HE'LL BE STRONG. HE'LL BE FAST. HE'LL BE VIRTUALLY INDESTRUC- TIBLE--

--AND HE'LL NEED THESE ADVANTAGES TO SURVIVE, MY DARLING.

GOODBYE, MY SON. GO BACK AND CHANGE THE WORLD SO THAT WE MIGHT NOT BECOME THIS *COLD, COMPLACENT* LOT...

"...GO BACK AND BRING A LITTLE *LIGHT* TO OUR LIVES AGAIN."

THE UKRAINE,
RUSSIA, 1938:

END

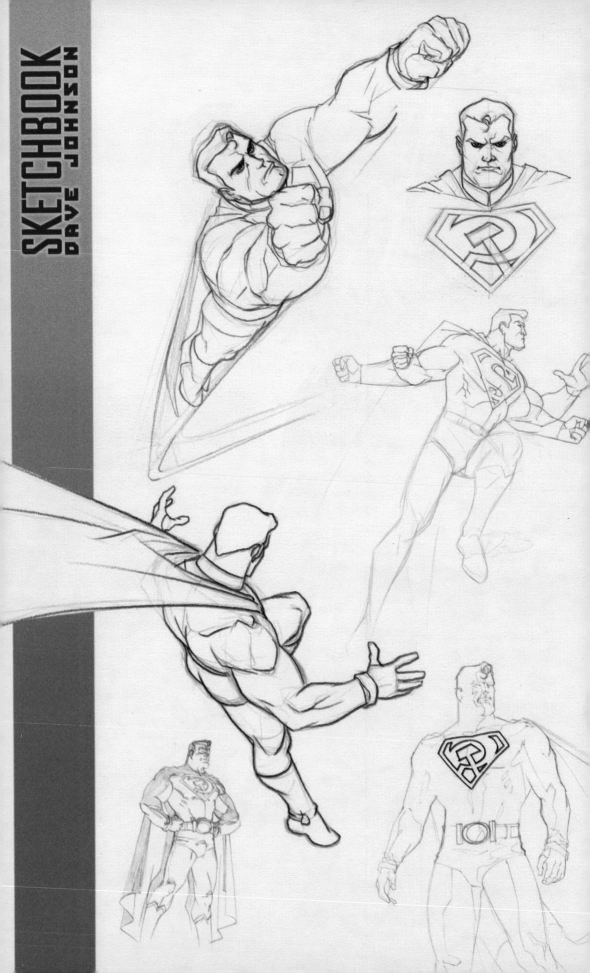

BOOK ONE

BOOK THREE

RED

RED

BOOK TWO

If I had finished the
Book, this would have
been Supes costume.
I still
like what KiLiAN
came up with, though.

BATMANKOFF w/ HAT!

Brown

GREY

JOHNSON 97

I took a lot of crap
from friends about this
Hat. But I still like the
design. RUSSIA is
cold. Why can't Batman
have a warm hat?

40% GREY

WHITE

DARK RED

40% GREY

AD LAYOUT FOR PAINTING

Here's two different ways to do the same shot. I think both work but a choice had to be made.
The final version had to be done with 5 point perspective. It's a real pain to do, but worth the effort.

unlike most artists I like to do most of my work on scrap paper then lightbox the final design on the bristol board. Maybe thats why I'm so slow. But it eliminates the pressure of having to get it right on the page the first time. not to mention I can enlarge or reduce the layout to suit my needs before I commit it to paper.

This was the first cover Idea for issue 3. But I felt it didn't fill up the space on the cover. Too much dead area on either side of the figure. Especially after reducing him down to fit under the Title logo. Well, at least it's SEEing the light of day in this book.

AHHH. The Devilpig. This little bastard has been showing up everywhere. Coming to a 100 Bullets cover soon.

THE RING ITSELF IS PRETTY MUCH THE SAME

GREEN LANTERN

?

_ IT'S A FLIGHT-SUIT KIND OF THING

GREEN

WHITE

GREEN LANTERN

GREEN

PRUSSIAN BLUE?

HIGHER BOOTS + GLOVES.

SUPERMAN
THE NEVER-ENDING BATTLE CONTINUES IN
THESE BOOKS FROM TITAN BOOKS:

GRAPHIC NOVELS

SON OF SUPERMAN
H. Chaykin/D. Tischman/
J.H. Williams III/M. Gray

SUPERMAN: END OF THE CENTURY
Stuart Immonen/José Marzan Jr.

SUPERMAN: INFINITE CITY
Mike Kennedy/Carlos Meglia

SUPERMAN: IT'S A BIRD
Steven T. Seagle/Teddy Kristiansen

SUPERMAN: SECRET IDENTITY
Kurt Busiek/S. Immonen

SUPERMAN: TRUE BRIT
Kim 'Howard' Johnson/John Cleese/John Byrne/Mark Farmer

COLLECTIONS

ALL-STAR SUPERMAN
Grant Morrison/Frank Quitely

KINGDOM COME
Mark Waid/Alex Ross

SUPERMAN: BACK IN ACTION
K. Busiek/F. Nicieza/P. Woods

SUPERMAN: BIRTHRIGHT
M. Waid/Leinil Francis Yu

SUPERMAN: CAMELOT FALLS
Vols. 1-2
K. Busiek/Carlos Pacheco

SUPERMAN CHRONICLES
Vols. 1-3
Jerry Siegel/Joe Schuster & Various

SUPERMAN: CRITICAL CONDITION
Various writers and artists

SUPERMAN: DAY OF DOOM
Dan Jurgens & Bill Sienkiewicz

THE DEATH AND RETURN OF SUPERMAN
Various writers and artists

SUPERMAN: EMPEROR JOKER
Various writers and artists

SUPERMAN: ENDGAME
Various writers and artists

SUPERMAN FOR ALL SEASONS
Jeph Loeb/Tim Sale

SUPERMAN: FOR TOMORROW
Vols. 1-2
Brian Azzarello/Jim Lee

SUPERMAN: GODFALL
Michael Turner/Joe Kelly/Talent Caldwell/Jason Gorder

SUPERMAN: INFINITE CRISIS
Various writers and artists

SUPERMAN: IN THE NAME OF GOG
Various writers and artists

SUPERMAN: NO LIMITS!
Various writers and artists

SUPERMAN: OUR WORLDS AT WAR Vols. 1 & 2
Various writers and artists

SUPERMAN: PRESIDENT LEX
Various writers and artists

SUPERMAN RETURNS: THE MOVIE AND OTHER TALES OF THE MAN OF STEEL
Various writers and artists

SUPERMAN RETURNS: THE PREQUEL
Various writers and artists

SUPERMAN: RETURN TO KRYPTON
Various writers and artists

SUPERMAN: RUIN REVEALED
Greg Rucka/Karl Kerschl

SUPERMAN: SACRIFICE
Various writers and artists

SUPERMAN: STRANGE ATTRACTORS
Gail Simone/J. Byrne/Nelson

SUPERMAN: THAT HEALING TOUCH
Various writers and artists

SUPERMAN: THE GREATEST STORIES EVER TOLD Vols. 1-2
Various writers and artists

SUPERMAN: THE JOURNEY
Mark Verheiden/Ed Benes/Tony Daniel

SUPERMAN: THE MAN OF STEEL Vols. 1-5
J. Byrne/M. Wolfman/J. Ordway

SUPERMAN: THE WRATH OF GOG
Chuck Austen/Ivan Reis

SUPERMAN: THEY SAVED LUTHOR'S BRAIN
Various writers and artists

SUPERMAN: 'TIL DEATH DO US PART
Various writers and artists

SUPERMAN: UP, UP AND AWAY!
Geoff Johns/K. Busiek/P. Woods

SUPERMAN: UNCONVENTIONAL WARFARE
Various writers and artists

SUPERMAN/ALIENS
Dan Jurgens/Kevin Nowlan

SUPERMAN/TARZAN: SONS OF THE JUNGLE
C. Dixon/C. Meglia

SUPERMAN VS. PREDATOR
David Michelinie/Alex Maleev

SUPERMAN VS. THE REVENGE SQUAD
Various writers and artists